HiM

His Infernal Majesty

HIM

His Infernal Majesty

Reinhardt Haydn

Plexus, London

For Anna Jones

Copyright © 2007 by Plexus Publishing Limited
Published by Plexus Publishing Limited
25 Mallinson Road
London SW11 1BW
www.plexusbooks.com
First Printing

British Library Cataloguing in Publication Data

Haydn, Reinhardt
  H.I.M. : His Infernal Majesty
  1. HIM (Heavy metal group) 2. Rock musicians - Finland -
  Biography
  I. Title
  782.4'2166'0922

  ISBN-10: 0-85965-392-7
  ISBN-13: 9780-85965-392-3

Cover photo by Paul Harries
Book and cover design by Rebecca Longworth
Printed in Spain by Vivapress, Barcelona

CONTENTS

I BLACK sun RISING

Music is my god, and is the only love that has never left me.
– Ville Valo

In the quarter century since the likes of Black Sabbath, Led Zeppelin, Deep Purple and Blue Cheer defined the genre, heavy metal had represented many things: excitement, rebellion, freedom, escapism, sex. Heavy metal was the sonic fury, bristles, studs and warts of Motorhead, the excess and sleaze of Mötley Crüe, the post-glam pout of Twisted Sister or W.A.S.P., the Satanic malevolence of Venom and a thousand other denim 'n' leather textures formed from loud guitars, pounding rhythms and coruscating vocals.

The heavy metal kids have had many faces, but before HIM, none of them represented perfect beauty. This exquisite splendour is evident in the striking good looks of their charismatic vocalist Ville Valo, the melancholy conviction of his lyrics and the seeping grandeur of the band's music. HIM are an anomalous phenomenon that defies easy categorisation. Their accessible, wide-screen rock transcends genres and has attracted a diverse following drawn from fans of heavy metal, gothic rock and pop. In an age where publicity and marketing demands that 'product' appeals to rigidly structured, preconceived demographics, HIM are a strange and wonderful mutation; atypical, unique.

As a means of defining their ethos, image and sound to an often uncomprehending media, HIM have fabricated their very own sub-genre: love metal. 'When we started out with the band in '94 or whatever, we started to call ourselves "love metal" because people had trouble categorising what we did.'

Ville Valo – The high priest of love metal.

'It's a tongue-in-cheek sort of thing,' Ville explained to *NME* journalist Dan Silver. 'We've got more sentimentality in our music than most of the metal acts, and our songs are not based on hate, but on love – so that sounded funny – and it shows that we can laugh at ourselves.'

As descriptive terms go, 'love metal' is an adequate summation of what HIM do. Similarly, the terms 'Goth'n'roll' and 'Scandinavian blues' have also been applied to the band. Irrespective of whatever subjective terms are applied to HIM, the simple fact is that they are a group who acknowledge, interpret and apply a staggeringly broad range of influences – from the pastoral sensitivity of Cat Stevens to the post-apocalyptic maelstrom of 1980s anarcho-punks Discharge. And in doing so, HIM create a new, inspiring *gestalt* that has won the band a devoted global following.

The story of HIM is that of a group of young men who simply loved music rather than seeing it as a career option; a band without a five-year plan, marketing strategy or target audience. 'We had no idea where it would lead us in the end,' observed Ville. 'Whether it would turn out to be silly psychedelic music or the meanest motherfucker of metal known to man. But it felt really good. We just incorporated all the elements that came naturally and took it from there. With pretty mediocre success, of course.' In order to understand how HIM achieved the success to which their frontman refers in such typically self-effacing terms, it is necessary to trace the roots of the band from their source.

Just before half past eight on the morning of 22 November 1976, Anita Valo gave birth to her first child: a boy named (but never christened) Ville Hermanni. 'Finnish people are not that religious,' Ville explained to *Rock Sound* in 2004. 'I haven't been baptised – I'm really proud of it. My mother belonged to the Lutheran church, my daddy wasn't baptised so they wanted me to have the option.' Although both Anita and Ville's father, Kari, were Finnish nationals, his mother was one of a significant number of Finns whose ancestry could be traced back to Hungary – the two countries share common (Finno-Ugric) linguistic traits dating back some 5000 years, and many Hungarians relocated to Finland after their homeland was stripped of two-thirds of its territory, following the signing of the Treaty of Trianon at the end of the First World War. It is from Anita that Ville inherited his dark good looks. 'My grandmother, who was of Hungarian/Romanian origins, did claim that we are descendants of Dracula,' Ville revealed. 'But she is dead now, and I can't ask her about that anymore. I am doing some research on it, because it would be very cool to be a relative of a vampire.'

The Valo family lived in a modest timber house in Vallila, a working class residential district just north of Helsinki. A traditional market town, Vallila's central square was featured in *Leningrad Cowboys Go America* director Aki Kaurismäki's 2002 drama, *Man Without A Past*.

Shortly after Ville's birth, Kari, who worked as a cab driver, relocated the family to a three room apartment in Oulunkylä, a small town that was engulfed by the Helsinki conurbation just after World War II. The suburb was best known for being among the sites where Lenin lived in hiding from the Tsarist police during the first decade of the twentieth century. Oulunkylä is a pleasant, modern district bordered to the east by the River Vantaa and surrounded by woodland. It was here that Ville spent his entire childhood and adolescence.

Like most babies, Ville was prone to tearful outbursts. His parents quickly devised a technique to stop this that provided their howling offspring with an introduction to music: 'When I was a baby and started to cry, my father used to play the song "Paratiisi" [Paradise] by Rauli "Badding" Somerjoki. Then he put me on his lap and started dancing. And I stopped crying.' In 1999, Ville would record 'Paratiisi' with Finnish folk rockers the Agents.

Kari and Anita shared a diverse taste in music that was inherited by their son; in addition to traditional Finnish artists such as Tapio Rautavaara, Hiski Salomaa and Tuomari Nurmio, the couple also owned records by J. J. Cale, Elvis Presley, the Rolling Stones, John Lee Hooker, Bo Diddley and Cat Stevens. 'Most of those records were OK,' observed Ville. 'Thank God my parents were no Finnish pop music fans.'

I've gotten my verbal acrobatics from my dad, and that's how I win people over. – Ville Valo

Ville's first interests were his teddy bear, Tyller – who Ville recalls suffered regular soakings ''cos I used to wet myself when I was young,' and Sami – an abandoned dog that Ville's parents had taken in. 'He was my role model,' recalled Ville. 'The dog taught me how to walk, but didn't teach me to shit all over the place.' Sami was just one of a menagerie of pets in the Valo household, which also included fish and turtles. When Sami died, Ville took the news very badly and developed a psychosomatic asthmatic reaction to dogs that persists to this day.

By the time he was two years old Ville was ready for his musical debut at a family party. The Valos had a friend named Jallu who was an enthusiastic Elvis Presley impersonator. At the height of Jallu's rendition of 'Are You Lonesome Tonight', Ville crawled across the floor in his baby-gro and picked up a small pair of his father's bongos from beside a pile of albums. Seizing both the drums and the moment, Ville began hammering out a lively accompaniment that gave the first indication of what would become his overriding passion in life. 'When I heard Elvis Presley, then I knew I had to do music,' he explained.

Two years later, when the family were visiting Jallu, Ville was terrified by the posters of Iron Maiden's mascot Eddie that adorned Jallu's son's bedroom. 'It was evening and dark and his room was full of Iron Maiden posters,' explained Ville. 'I got scared shitless and ran away. Maybe, even today, I'm still afraid of Eddie – just a tiny bit. I had to get over my fear so I could later like Iron Maiden.' Despite fleeing in horror, a fascination with the dark side of popular culture began to take root in Ville's mind. 'When Ville is very young, he liked very much Star Wars toys and Darth Vader is very near his heart,' recalled Kari.

As his personality began to form, it quickly became apparent that Ville was a highly imaginative and creative child. He began listening to the radio and his parents' records, often to the exclusion of other pursuits. 'When he was five or six,' Kari explained, 'I pushed him in sport, but he was interested more and more in music.'

His young imagination also received a turbo-charged boost from literature. 'My parents read almost everything to me – sometimes the Arabian fairy tales of *1001 Nights*, but mostly *Grimm's Fairy Tales*,' Ville told *Rennbahn Express* in May 2000. 'That's why I became so crazy. Those stories are mostly about murder and manslaughter, sadism and massacre.'

When Ville was six years old, he was delighted to hear that he was not destined to remain an only child. 'Back in 1982, I got some socks from my ma,' he recalled. 'She always buys me socks and underwear. After we had Christmas dinner and gave the presents away, my ma said that I was going to have a little brother. It was just a great thing to happen.' Jesse was born the following year and like his big bro' – who subsequently earned a green belt – took to being enrolled in judo classes with great enthusiasm. 'When we were younger we fought like cats and dogs,' Ville explained in 2001. 'He does Thai boxing – he won the Finnish championships twice, so he is pretty tough.'

In Finland, formal education begins in the year that a child has his or her seventh birthday. In keeping with his creative nature, Ville was enrolled at a school where there was specific emphasis on music. However, Ville's 'crazy' streak soon manifested. He was regularly involved in fights with the other children and was moved from one class to another in an attempt to pacify him. When this failed, he was sent for a brain scan in order to determine whether any particular neurological disorder was causing him to be uncontrollable. Eventually, it was discovered that allowing him to exercise his hyperactive imagination through drawing brought about an improvement in behaviour. 'I am insane because of this genetic disorder in me. I am half my mum and half my dad: My dad is a really calm, thinking type of person. My mum is the total opposite – very temperamental. She gets angry very easily,' explained Ville. 'My dad always told me that money doesn't grow on trees, so I'm careful. My mum told me not to put my fingers in electrical sockets – so I did.'

Fortunately, Ville survived electrocution and in 1984 experienced the musical epiphany that would set him on the path to rock'n'roll damnation and global fame. Keen to begin acquiring a record collection, he bought his first album – Kiss's *Animalize* – at the recommendation of his cousin Pia. The post-glam quartet's loud-but-accessible take on heavy metal, epitomised by the young Finn's favourite track

I've never been truly, madly in love. I think I'm too young for it. – Ville Valo

The mid 1990s incarnation of HIM: Pätkä, Linde, Ville and Mige.

'Heaven's on Fire', instantly enraptured Ville. 'I started my music career because of Kiss, more exactly because of Gene Simmons, because of the blood and the fire.'

It was the influence of Gene Simmons that prompted Ville to take up bass guitar when he was ten years old. His parents found him an SG Gibson copy and stumped up the funds for some lessons. Kari, who had recently given up taxi driving in favour of running a sex shop, was insistent that Ville apply himself to practicing. 'It was always important to him that I do my guitar lessons,' Ville told *Bravo* magazine. 'I wasn't allowed to go out until I had done them.'

'I still remember that I got more pain than pleasure from that bass and the first small amp. My fingers were terribly sore, but still my mother said, "now practice god-dammit," recalled Ville. 'I don't know if my mum wanted me to become a musician, but still it was good that she forced me to practice. This way I learned a lot, even though the practicing bored me like hell. I never played the piano and I have no other classical basic knowledge. I preferred to learn how to play pop and rock instead of something of higher cultural value.'

Music for me is an emotional thing and it really does make me happy. It's not a tool for me to get fame or see my face in the papers or anything like that. It's about the fact that I really do enjoy it. – Ville Valo

In addition to practicing his bass, Ville began immersing himself in metal, seeking out much of Kiss's back catalogue and discovering bands such as W.A.S.P., Twisted Sister and Mötley Crüe. It was during this period that Ville's fantasies of becoming the next Gene Simmons or Nikki Sixx took a giant leap forward when he met the first of his future bandmates: Mikko Paananen – otherwise known as Mige.

Mikko Henrik Julius Paananen was almost two years Ville's senior, having been born in Helsinki on 19 December 1974. His parents were both highly creative; his mother, Riitta, was an actress and pianist who had appeared at the National Theatre in Helsinki, as well as on TV and radio, while his father, Sven played oboe and cor anglais in the Helsinki Philharmonic Orchestra. Riitta's father, Ossi Elstelä, was an actor, director and writer who appeared in around 40 films between 1937 and 1962.

Mige's early years were spent in Oulunkylä with his parents and older brother. Unsurprisingly, he was surrounded by music from an early age, but tended to rebel against the discipline required to learn an instrument to a classical level – instead, like Ville, he settled on the bass guitar, which he describes as 'a very underestimated instrument'. Although he initially listened to hip-hop courtesy of his older broth-

Their Satanic majesties relax – HIM chill out amid suitably bohemian bibelots.

er, Mige's favourite band was, and remains, Black Sabbath. Sabbath bassist Geezer Butler drew Mige's attention in much the same way that Gene Simmons had struck a power chord with Ville. 'My pops bought me a Cort bass – kind of a Steinberger copy,' Mige recalled. 'I broke it on stage while playing with my high school band.'

One of the main reasons why the two youngsters bonded was their shared enthusiasm for the bass. 'I met Mige when I was in third grade, when I started playing bass, Ville confirmed. 'He was in fifth grade then. Because Mige also had a bass, we hung around quit a lot, but we just spent all the time playing our basses.' In addition to rock, the duo shared an interest in horror films. 'We started hanging around together when I borrowed some eighties gore films from him,' recalled Mige. 'I know it's not the coolest way to start a friendship but we got into some more creative things eventually – like sitting by the river smoking pot.'

I used to be a gardener. I loved that – the worst part of it was picking up the turds. – Mige Amour

When Mige was thirteen, his parents divorced and he went to live with his mother in Tuusula, a scenic municipality about 30 kilometres north of Helsinki, which had once been the home of the composer Johann Sibelius. This relocation meant that he saw less of Ville, but their friendship endured. 'He was a freak, who used to wear two different shoes, with incredibly long filthy hair and incredibly ugly clothes and had the strangest friends,' laughed Ville. 'We are so different, that we can never envy each other for anything. We're both very balanced, but in a different, really bizarre way.'

In 1989, Ville had started the upper stage of his compulsory education when he met Linde, who had recently transferred from another school. 'I was in seventh grade when I met Linde. I went to the school on the border between East Pakila and Oulunkylä and Linde was going to the same school. Because he was guitarist and I was bassist, we sometimes played together,' explained Ville. 'Linde was already the same hopeless guy as today. Maybe he is even more introverted today, as silent as a talking man can be.'

Otherwise known as Mikko Viljami Lindstrom, Linde was only a few months older than Ville, having been born on 12 August 1976 in Klaukkala – a small town in the Nurmijavi district, about 30 kilometres north of Helsinki. His father was an engineer and his mother worked for FinnAir, the national airline. Linde was an introverted boy notable only for his bobbed blond hair and glasses. 'When I was in the kindergarten, other kids use to tease me cause I had glasses . . . They called me "linssi" – its Finnish for "lens" but I have gotten over it now. I hope.'

Like Ville and Mige, Linde had developed a passion for music at an early age; his

Mige Amour – Bass titan and hygiene hazard.

parents encouraged him to buy his first record when he was only six – the album *Känkkäränkkä Ja Koko Muu Konkkaronkka* by wholesome Finnish country/folk vocalist Mikko Alatalo, who later went on to become a member of the Finnish parliament. Four years later they bought their son his first guitar as a Christmas present – a scaled down acoustic hand made by the Finnish company Landola. 'I started to take lessons immediately,' recalled Linde.

Linde's first guitar hero was Steve Vai, the axe virtuoso who came to prominence through his work with Frank Zappa and David Lee Roth. 'I used to listen a lot to the albums he did with the David Lee Roth Band and my favourites from his solo albums were *Flex-Able* and *Passion And Warfare*. I used to adore him to the point that when I finally saw him play live in Kulttuuritalo, Helsinki, I felt like a hysterical little girl trying not to faint or have a heart attack.'

From the outset, Linde was aware of the technicalities of his chosen instrument and tended to gravitate toward the most accomplished players. 'Jimi Hendrix is a genius and very talented musically. I don't own many of his albums but I love to watch his concerts on video,' he explained. 'I had nightmares for a couple of weeks after I first saw his Woodstock performance as a kid.'

> *One of my long term goals is to learn to react in real time.* – Linde Lindström

Over the next year or so, Ville divided his time between jamming with Linde and other school friends, widening his palette of influences to include the likes of Led Zeppelin, Iggy and the Stooges, Deep Purple, Neil Young and Cat Stevens, attending school and working in his father's sex shop.

As holiday or weekend jobs go, working in a sex shop is a world away from the usual paper round or stint serving up flaccid fast food. However, as Kari had been running the shop for five years, Ville took the experience very much in his stride.

'In the beginning, it was exiting just because it was new,' he remembers. 'Would there be another box with bizarre things in the hall again? I played with dildos like they were cars . . . I mean, what's the difference between selling bananas or dildos? OK you put them in a different hole – but it all comes down to the same thing.'

Quickly adapting to his new role, Ville saw the job in an educational light. 'I thought it was a bit weird, but in the end it's paid off in many ways. It was a great way to educate myself sexually, because it's been free and basically very sixties.

'Everything was better than filling the shells in a grocery store. Not that I could interfere with the clients. For the first couple of weeks, I have to admit, I didn't have total control over my hormones. It takes some time to get used to naked women and

An early publicity shot of the band, featuring keyboardist Antto Melasniemi (far right).

flying sperm. Everywhere you look – sex, sex, sex.'

Ville also discovered that his new job required a strong stomach as well as an open mind, 'I once also had a man who wanted to return his fake vagina. Used and all. Wanted to trade it. Our reaction wasn't what he had expected. It was so disgusting it was almost funny.'

Another downside of Ville's part-time job was that his friends' parents took a dim view of such permissiveness and forbade their kids from hanging out with him. 'Everybody associates a sex shop automatically with something dirty and filthy,' observed Ville. 'Nobody was allowed to come to my house to play. It made me very sad. Our store isn't kinky: no kids, no animals or hardcore S&M. That's the house rule. We just sell the basic material. Eventually, my dad invited some of the parents home. I don't know exactly what he told them, but after that it was alright. Once I got into high school everybody wanted to come home with me. I was cool then. Free porn, right?'

Music's always been really cathartic. It's the best drug for me to get away from the everyday pressures just for a second via a good song. – Ville Valo

In addition to according him some anti-hero status among his high school chums, the sex shop also provided Ville with a degree of leverage over one of his teachers. 'One day suddenly my [male] physics teacher wanted to buy underwear for girlies. We both blushed totally when we recognised each other.'

While Ville concedes that 'too much pornography is not good for your mind', on the whole he found that the experience granted him some useful insights into human nature. 'There's a lot of psychology involved. That was a challenge for me. No client asks for advice openly. You have to read their eyes. Every client asks for a personal approach. With some you have to whisper, somebody else wants a serious conversation. One wrong word and they run out of the store.'

Notwithstanding his early exposure to adult literature, movies and artificial phalli, Ville enjoyed a fairly normal adolescence, discovering girls and alcohol in the normal way and passing through school without any major dramas. On the whole, his grades were good and, after a rocky start attributable to an overzealous teacher, he particularly excelled in maths. 'I always loved maths, solving a problem is a great challenge. I think mathematics is art to such an extent.' Ville also excelled at history, art and, unsurprisingly, music, but tended to view formal education as something of a waste of time. 'School should only be attended when one is ready to learn something. Like for example when you are 30 and really willing to study. School is just a necessary evil for all young people and everybody just hates it. You learn it all by heart without getting to the real meaning of things.'

The classic HIM line up: Emerson Burton (keyboards); Migé Paananen (bass); Ville Valo (vocals); Linde Lindström (guitar); Gas Lipstick (drums).

Aside from his dislike of school, Ville's adolescent growing pains were largely confined to a mild dose of obsessive/compulsive behaviour and a vituperative rebellion against his mother. 'When I was thirteen or fourteen years old I had a neurosis and I even had to wake up during the night to fix the angle of a fucking pen on a table. Everything had to be right there geometrically. Then I thought it's best to quit and be a messy slob.

'I went through a shitty adolescent phase, where I used to constantly call my mother a whore,' confessed Ville. 'My father forced me to write the word "whore" a thousand times, so I would understand what a bad word it was.' This enlightened and subtle approach to disciplining Ville was typical of Kari and Anita's progressive manner of parenting. 'My parents were really easy on me,' Ville confirmed. 'When I got drunk for the first time, they just laughed at me.'

Nothing is strange in the realm of sex. The only thing I don't like is people having sex with animals. You can never be sure whether they want to or not. – Ville Valo

One of the main reasons why, as a teenager, Ville avoided getting into serious trouble was that he was largely pre-occupied by music and, to a lesser extent, skating. These all-consuming obsessions also tempered his developing interest in the opposite sex. 'When my friends started to get interested in girls, I concentrated on music. I thought girls were scary and kinda useless.'

During his early teens, Ville preferred jamming with his friends to chasing girls; when he did meet someone he liked, he tended to view it as less than important. 'I was never the kind of guy to have steady relationships, and in my school years I had no real girlfriends. I just dated some girls sometimes.' He certainly didn't enjoy his first kiss. 'It was horrible! I still don't like French kisses – you know, with the tongue – and, well, she did. So, I wasn't very impressed.'

However, hormones being what they are, by the time he was fourteen, Ville had endured his first encounter with teenage love and the concomitant broken heart. 'She fell in love with my best friend and that was the time I wrote my first song. That changed my life a lot, well it changed everything.'

Ville's first song was written at around the same time he formed his first band with Linde, which was called B.L.O.O.D. – a name inspired by W.A.S.P.'s use of the acronym. 'We didn't have a singer and played Iron Maiden's "Run To The Hills" in front of the music class. We did it once or twice, and that was the end of that band.' Aside from lacking a vocalist, B.L.O.O.D. was mainly notable for having two drummers, although one of the duo was too nervous to perform in public and thus only appeared at rehearsals.

Like most teenagers who pick up a guitar and develop a passion for rock, Ville, Linde and Mige formed and split bands with various combinations of their friends on a regular basis. After B.L.O.O.D., Ville joined a band called the Elovena Boys (Elovena is the wholesome farm girl depicted on the packaging of popular brands of Finnish oatmeal). The band played covers of songs by U2 and Dire Straits, making around half a dozen appearances at school concerts.

Linde teamed up with Ville to form Kemoterapia in 1990; the band being essentially a duo with Ville supplying bass guitar and drums, while Linde played guitar. This group never performed live, but did work on original material such as Ville's ode to lost love, which he had written some months earlier.

Essentially a bedroom band, Kemoterapia morphed into Terapia, and then Winha, before Ville and Linde formed what could be considered their first band proper, in terms of writing songs and performing live: Aurora. This group featured Ville as drummer, with Lille supplying guitar as usual. The group were fronted by Erkki Lilja, who would subsequently go on to sing with Finnish pop rockers Ihmepoika who released their eponymous debut album in 2002.

Aurora – a quintet rounded out with Joonas Merikanto on second guitar and bassist Juha Marttinen – got off to a lively start. After rehearsing for several months they were ready to face the public. At one of their earliest gigs Erkki decided to prepare by drinking a whole bottle of 60 per cent proof Koskenkorva – a powerful Finnish vodka variant known as *viina* (hard liquor). Erkki made his stage entrance supported by his bandmates, and proceeded to collapse on the lighting supports – bringing the lighting rig crashing down around Ville's drum kit.

The band, which mixed original material with covers of rock standards such as Deep Purple's 'Smoke On The Water', Hendrix's 'Purple Haze' and 'Paranoid' by Black Sabbath, often had drinking at the top of their agenda. 'In junior high,' Ville explained, 'I had six or seven bands running at the same time and at least one rehearsal per day. There were the Jazz and Dixieland bands at school and also Aurora, which always meant beer in excess.'

In addition to the odd drunken stage imbroglio, Ville discovered the pitfalls of excessive drinking in his personal life. 'I was at a party and I ended up making out with my crush. I had drunk a few beers too much and I threw up in the bed. I don't think it was a right way to show my affection.'

Keen to broaden their partying opportunities, Ville and pals decided to organise some hippy parties at their school as a means of raising funds for a class trip to Amsterdam. However, despite having the permission of their class teacher, school director Martti Ilvonen had what Ville described as 'a kind of schizophrenic fit' and came charging into the main hall, declaring that 'no way was there going to be a hippy party in his school – because it was all about smoking hash.' Their plans scup-

Initially a reluctant frontman, Ville quickly developed one of the most magnetic stage presences in modern rock.

pered, Ville took revenge by composing a lively number entitled 'Martti Ilvonen Tunkee Kyrpää Suoleen', which roughly translates as 'Martti Ilvonen puts his dick up assholes.' 'We played that song at the autumn concert and all the other teachers laughed their heads off. People went completely crazy and started throwing chairs around. From then on we were forbidden to play at school concerts in Oulunkylä,' recalled Ville.

Despite this setback, the class trip went ahead – with funds being raised by selling doughnuts. The ten-day trek took Ville, Linde and Erkki through Sweden, Denmark and Germany *en route* to their destination and gave Aurora the opportunity to play a small number of shows once they reached Holland. Aurora's first show was in Utrecht, where the band got drunk and played what Ville described as 'some fucking Prog Jazz'.

Take showers and change your underwear: that can impress women. – Ville Vallo

Aside from a family holiday to Thailand, the Amsterdam trip was Ville's first experience of foreign travel. Ever the seeker of forbidden pleasures, Ville took the opportunity to visit one of Amsterdam's famous coffee shops and got righteously stoned.

While Aurora had been blazing a path to healthy doughnut sales and unhealthy excess, Mige had been visiting the USA. 'I went to the Berklee College of Music in Boston for one summer and during that period, I learned more than I did in a couple of years studying here in Finland. I was feeling a bit mentally unstable at that time but anyway I had a great time there.' On his return, the bassist – who had also been playing with such bands as Spirit Sauna, the Motherfuckers and the gloriously named Bullshit Ass – hooked up with Ville to form a new band. This time around they chose a name that Ville had discovered in Anton LaVey's *The Satanic Bible* – His Infernal Majesty.

Bare footed and badass – HIM go 'grrr' for the camera

2 CORPS CADAVER

When you do something, do it all the way.
– Ville Vallo

The first incarnation of HIM formed in late 1991 and played only one concert – on New Year's Eve of that year at the Semifinal Club in Helsinki. Instrumentally, His Infernal Majesty were an odd fish – Ville played a six-string bass in lieu of lead guitar, while Mige held down the bass parts. The duo was backed by Juippi, a drummer who would later resurface as a member of doom metallers Reverend Bizarre.

Juippi was later replaced by Juha Tarvonen and the group stuck together long enough to record a demo track, 'Xilqa Xilqa Besa Besa' under the name of Kafferi. The track subscquently formed the basis of a later demo, 'Borellus', and derives its title from *The Necronomicon,* a fictional book initially created by fantasy, horror and science-fiction author H. P. Lovecraft for his 1924 short story 'The Hound'. Ascribed to Lovecraft's 'mad Arab' Abdul Alhazred, the book became a central part of the author's elder gods mythos and described their history, as well as the incantations required to summon them. 'Xilqa Xilqa Besa Besa' was devised as a 'most excellent conjuration' to protect the user against hordes of demons. Ville also discovered the name 'Kafferi' from reading Lovecraft – however, once it was pointed out to him that it was a derivation of the racially offensive Afrikaans expression *kaffir*, it was immediately dropped.

In 1992 His Infernal Majesty recorded a seven-track demo, *Witches and Other Night Fears* – a title drawn from an essay by nineteenth century writer and poet Charles Lamb, which was used as an epigraph to Lovecraft's 1929 short story 'The Dunwich Horror'. The demo was not widely distributed and the only surviving copy is believed to reside within Ville's private collection.

Ville occupies the foreground with his usual stage props:
a cigarette and some booze.

Ville and Mige also found time to work on another project, Unga Kaskelottär – essentially a duo, in February 1992 they recorded a five-track demo at Sore Studios in the Sornäs district of Helsinki. Although this demo remains largely unheard, titles such as 'Fridge (Insalubrious Verrucose Uretha)' and 'Tribal Orchestration Covered By Purulent Discharge' hint that the boys were heading in an experimental direction, far removed from their later work.

Mige's musical development was sharply curtailed when he was called up for the two-year national service that all male citizens are liable for. 'At eighteen I was in the army,' he recalled. 'It gives you a little bit of spine – you get punished a bit every day but you actually enjoy it. It gives you a good attitude when you go back to society.'

> *We wanted to appeal to ourselves at first; there was no conscious effort to be anything, we just played what we liked. – Ville Vallo*

With Mige indisposed, Ville joined another band, the Donits-Osmo Experience, a progressive underground rock outfit that included brother and sister Joel and Vilma Melasniemi on guitar and vocals. In addition to being the cousins of Antto Melasniemi, who would subsequently become HIM's keyboard player, Joel and Vilma's parents, Eero Melasniemi and Kristiina Halkola, were both experienced actors with many film and television appearances to their credits. After the Donits-Osmo Experience disbanded, Vilma would follow in their footsteps and appear in several TV series and art house films, whereas Joel would later resurface with the popular musicians collective Ultra Bra, who represented Finland in the 1998 Eurovision Song Contest with their hit song 'Tyttöjen välisestä ystävyydestä' (About Friendship Between Girls).

Ville played just one notable gig with the Experience, supporting grunge behemoths Mudhoney at the Lepakko Club in Helsinki on 27 April 1992. The group also recorded several demos and contributed two tracks, 'Cypress Creek' and 'Killfuck', to the 23-track sampler album *Rumba 10 – A Collection Of Fresh Finnish Underground Rock*. Sonically, the Donits-Osmo Experience resembles the bass-heavy 'psychedelic polka' of Les Claypool's California based trio Primus, complete with irregular time changes and Ville's swooping bass lines.

Away from music, after leaving school in 1992, Ville enrolled in evening art classes in Käpylä, which he gave up after about a year and a half, on account of being fed up with studying in general and the long bus journey required to get there. 'My parents probably were disappointed when I quit school,' he observed.

When he was eighteen, Ville left home after his family adopted a Great Dane

HIM try out some soft furnishings – former keyboard player Juska Salminen is on the far right.

named Fido who had been mistreated by his previous owner. The dog caused Ville's asthma to resurface – a situation exacerbated by the fact he had stopped taking his medication, because it had been such a long time since he'd had any kind of attack. In fact, the attack was so bad that Ville had to be rushed to hospital where he spent a fortnight in a ward generally reserved for lung cancer patients. As a birthday present, Kari rented his son a small apartment in 'a posh area' just south of Bulevardi in central Helsinki, where Ville could recuperate without being affected by dog hairs and other irritants. 'It was an incredible feeling to move into your own place,' recalled Ville. 'One didn't need to fear the toilet door would open while masturbating, and one could sleep whenever he wanted, listen to music or play it, whenever one felt like it. This was real freedom.'

I don't have time for dreaming because I have to work hard to make my dreams come true. –Ville Valo

In addition to providing him with a home of his own, Ville's asthma also ensured that he could not be considered for national service. Although this disappointed Kari, it at least ensured that Ville could concentrate on his music. This initially took the form of lashing together a fresh demo with Linde. Checking into a four-track studio in Helsinki's Lepakko youth centre, they recorded three tracks: 'Borellus' (the reworking of 'Xilqa Xilqa Besa Besa'), 'Serpent Ride' – another Lovecraft influenced track that features a quotation from his 1936 novella *The Shadow Over Innsmouth* and 'The Heartless', a track that would be reworked several times, becoming a cornerstone of the initial trio of HIM releases between 1995-97. For these recordings Ville supplied vocals and drums, while Linde played guitar and bass.

By 1995, Mige had completed his national service and was among the first to hear the demo. He was immediately entranced by the powerful, melodic nature of the tracks and impressed by the musical leap forward his friends had made over the past two years. Realising that they needed to form a proper group in order to do the songs justice, Mige readily agreed to hook up with Ville and Linde and the trio set to work rehearsing and seeking out a drummer.

During the summer, Ville, Linde and Mige made a visit to the Tavastia Club, Helsinki's premier rock venue and still the best place to catch upcoming local bands alongside visiting acts from abroad. 'We chill out at Tavastia very often,' Ville told *Bravo* magazine in March 2000. 'The Club has got a little bar, where you can get some food too, and there are always good rock bands playing there.'

On this occasion, local grunge metal outfit Slumgudgeon were on the bill. Ville and company where hugely impressed with the style and technique of their drummer

Mige and Ville offer up a practical demonstration of love metal.

Pätkä and obtained his phone number from Jimsonweed frontman Suho Superstar, who was friendly with both the His Infernal Majesty and Slumgudgeon camps.

Although Ville was initially uncertain about ringing Pätkä as he had never invited anyone to join a band who hadn't already been a personal friend, it was obvious that the drummer would be ideal for His Infernal Majesty and the group desperately needed to bring their numbers up to a full quota in order to play live. After receiving the phone call, Pätkä cycled over to meet Ville and once he had listened to the demo agreed to join.

A good meal is anything with a lot of grease and salt. – Linde Lindström

Juhana Tuomas Rantala was born in Tampere, Finland's third largest city, on 11 February 1974. He acquired the nickname Pätkä on account of his hanging out with his friend Pekka – Pekka and Pätkä being a famous Finnish comedy duo played by actors Mauri Kuosmanen and Jaako Kalio, who featured in Visa Mäkinen's mid 1980s films *Pekka & Pätkä ja tuplajättipotti* and *Pekka Puupää poliisina*. Pätkä's family left Tampere when he was very young and moved south east to the college town of Riihimäki, before relocating again to the city of Lappeentanta, which lies in the south-east of Finland, about 30 kilometres from the Russian border. It was here that Pätkä spent much of his youth and developed his talent as a drummer, before leaving home to form Slumgudgeon in 1992. Since then, Pätkä had been dividing his time between his band and a job at a municipal company that administered local bus services and conditions of carriage.

Although Pätkä's decision to join His Infernal Majesty effectively spelt the end for Slumgudgeon – who were pretty well established, having released two albums on Finnish label Stupido Twin Records (1992's *And On What Grounds* and *Factoraped* in 1995) – the drummer thought highly enough of his new band and their demo to take the risk of starting from square one. In order to get things moving, Pätkä organised the band's first proper rehearsal space at Tapanila, a district in northeast Helsinki which lies about twenty minutes by train from the city centre.

On nineteenth December 1995, the new band made their live debut at the Teatro club in Helsinki. 'My brother owned it and I was working there so we just went and supported a famous Finnish singer/songwriter – Kauko Röyhkä – without asking permission,' explained Mige. The performance bordered on the disastrous, with His Infernal Majesty's unbilled appearance going down poorly with a crowd who had turned out to enjoy Röyhkä's more sedate sound. Additionally, Mige's dodgy re-wiring of the club's public address system continually broke down – 'that's what you

Guitarist Linde, a.k.a. Lily Lazer, a.k.a. Daniel Lioneye – the driving force behind HIM's majestic sound.

call "a bummer" in English speaking countries,' opined Mige.

Ville also found his first experience of singing to a live audience somewhat bowel-loosening. 'I felt like I was going to shit my pants. I was always afraid to sing because I was shy and I was meant to be the bass player. I'm still afraid but they make me do it. After a couple of beers, I'm fine. Before, when I played bass, I was at the back somewhere, laughing my ass off. Now I am up front.'

Undaunted, His Infernal Majesty opted to view the episode as a learning experience, and returned to the Teatro stage just over a week later to perform a selection of songs by American doom metallers Type O Negative. A feature of Type O Negative's sound was Josh Silver's keyboards and synth effects; in order to replicate this for the concert, His Infernal Majesty drafted in Janne Johannes Puurtinen, a.k.a. King Tut. A friend of Mige's, Janne, would go on to establish himself in bands such as Cosmos Tango, Sub-Urban Tribe and Torpedo, before rejoining HIM as Emerson Burton in 2001.

This time around, His Infernal Majesty placed themselves in front of a far more receptive audience than had been the case supporting Kauko Röyhkä – they shared the bill with cello metal ensemble Apocalyptica, a trio of Sibelius Academy graduates who were making their live debut and would subsequently sell more than two million albums worldwide, featuring orchestral arrangements of songs by Metallica, Faith No More and Pantera among others. In 2004 Ville would provide guest vocals, along with Rasmus frontman Lauri Ylönen, for the Apocalyptica single 'Bittersweet'. On the night, the small club was packed and the audience gave both bands a hugely enthusiastic reception. In addition to providing Ville and the band with some welcome encouragement, the performance demonstrated the value of rounding out their developing sound with the addition of keyboards.

The need for keyboards was further underlined when the band came to record their second demo, featuring a version of Chris Isaak's 1989 single 'Wicked Game', which had become a transatlantic top ten hit after being featured in David Lynch's 1990 twisted take on the road movie genre, *Wild At Heart*. In order to replicate the sound of rainfall to add some additional atmosphere to the track Antto Einari Melasniemi was brought in to provide the necessary synthesized embellishments. A friend of Ville's since the vocalist's time with the Donits-Osmo Experience, Antto was a multi-instrumentalist who would retain a loose association with His Infernal Majesty prior to becoming a full member at the start of 1997.

Also included on the second demo were two original compositions, 'Stigmata Diaboli' – which would be subsequently reworked as 'Sigillum Diaboli' and included on the American and German editions of *Razorblade Romance* – and 'The Phantom Gate', from which lyrical elements would be recycled for the track 'Your Sweet 666' in 1997.

*There's always reasons to make mistakes.
Because then you do new mistakes next time. So
they're beautiful mistakes. – Ville Valo*

His Infernal Majesty made their third appearance at the Teatro club in April 1996, where their set was centred around cover versions of songs originally recorded by Danish satanic shock-rocker King Diamond. Two months later, the band made their debut at the 1,000 capacity Tavastia supporting Jimsonweed. By this time, the quartet of Ville, Mige, Linde and Pätkä was gradually supplanting their corpus of Type O Negative, Kiss and W.A.S.P. covers with original material and the group felt confident enough to enter the studio to record their first genuine release.

This was largely facilitated by BMG Finland executive Asko Kallonen, who discovered His Infernal Majesty's second demo among a pile of submissions that had been sent to his office. These days best known for his role as the jury chairman on the Finnish version of the *Pop Idol* franchise, Kallonen was impressed with the group's 'nice' version of 'Wicked Game' and felt that Ville's voice had a lot of potential. Kallonen thought that His Infernal Majesty would be a suitable band to help establish his label's new Terrier imprint, and got in touch with the group. 'A week later a guy with a weird hippie fur coat came into the office at our request,' Kallonen told *Suosikki* magazine. 'He was smoking the whole time . . . His answers to all my questions were either "I don't know" or "I don't care."'

A vastly experienced promoter and publicist, Kallonen wasn't fazed by Ville's uncommunicative manner, although he subsequently admitted to being slightly taken aback by the remainder of the band: 'The bassist could walk around a city in just his underpants, the drummer wore sneakers with the soles falling off and the guitarist didn't say anything ever.' Irrespective of his initial surprise at the group's individual style and demeanour, Kallonen was convinced by His Infernal Majesty's 'combination of romance and danger' and gave the band their first recording contract.

In the late summer of 1996, His Imperial Majesty spent five days in Helsinki's Finnvox recording studio laying down tracks for a four-track debut E.P. Established in 1965, Finnvox was Finland's first purpose-built professional recording facility and is now firmly established as the country's premier studio. The sessions were produced by Hiili Hiilesmaa who had met Ville the previous year while playing with his own band the Skreppers, who would go on to become one of HIM's favourite support acts.

New versions of 'Wicked Game', 'Stigmata Diaboli', and 'The Heartless' were recorded for the EP, as well as a new song 'Dark Sekret Love' which would resurface on the German edition of the 'Join Me' single in 1999. All four tracks clearly demonstrate the way in which the band would establish a template of combining Black Sabbath style riffage with ephemeral layers of echoing vocals and chorus-drenched guitar. Their sound was further enhanced by the addition of a rhythm guitarist named Oki who had also played in the Lappeenranta based thrash metal group, Charged. Oki's tenure with His Infernal Majesty came to an abrupt end when he became overly interested in Pätkä's girlfriend and was expelled from the group having never played with them live.

Released on 19 October 1996, the *666 Ways To Love: Prologue* EP was a limited pressing of 1,000 copies, supplied in a digipack featuring a 1960s image of Ville's mother, Anita on the cover and a moody blue-lit picture of Ville and the (obscured) band on the inlay.

The band celebrated their debut release with a gig at the Tavastia club on the day the disc came out and within days Finnish radio had picked up on His Infernal Majesty's version of 'Wicked Game' to such an extent that despite the small number of discs made available to the public, the EP climbed into the national Top Ten and remained on the chart until the new year. Although the band shot a home made video for 'Wicked Game', directed by Antto which saw the band taking a dog for a stroll in a public park, the clip was not widely seen until it appeared on the *Love Metal Archives Volume 1* DVD. Reflecting on his choice of cover version in an interview with *Kerrang!*'s Emma Johnston, Ville observed, 'We've always played lots of cover tunes – by Madonna and Ramones and all sorts of weird acts. It just felt good, that's the reason why we did it.'

*Our drummer only knows how to talk about his drums' mark, the keyboard player only knows about dance and techno music, and our guitar player is a mute. – **Ville Valo***

Equally celebratory was the group's final gig of 1996 – establishing a tradition that had its roots in their very first concert, they played a New Years' Eve show at the Teatro where they added songs by synth-goths Depeche Mode, Raul 'Badding' Somerjoki and other 'pop classics' to a fun evening that saw them supported by the Rasmus and progressive metal outfit Kyyria – whose drummer Mika Karpinnen would replace Antto in HIM two and a half years later.

The New Year's Eve gig brought His Infernal Majesty to the attention of public relations executive Silke Yli-Sirniö, who's reaction to seeing Ville was 'Shit – is this the reincarnation of Jim Morrison, or what?' Silke was connected to German music publishers and promoters Drakkar Entertainment who had links with the successful GUN Records imprint as well as BMG Germany. She approached the band with the suggestion of hooking them up with a record contract outside of Finland and was ultimately instrumental in securing the group's contract with BMG Germany.

The buzz that had suddenly sprung up in the wake of the *666 Ways To Love: Prologue* EP's domestic chart success was now matched by the type of support and promotion infrastructure that a modern group needs in order to function. In addition to Asko Kallonen and Silke, the group were also benefiting from representation by

Ville with manager Seppo Vesterinen, whose vast music biz experience has proven invaluable throughout the band's career.

Tiina Vuorinen, who had carved out a formidable reputation promoting and organising tours for Hanoi Rocks and would become a central figure in arranging the band's first tours. 'She seemed like a very dubious swindler,' laughed Ville. 'She had all these mannerisms that indicated that she had seen the world – we were in shock in the beginning.' Tiina was also the ex-wife of Hanoi Rocks manager Seppo Vesterinen, who was immediately impressed with His Infernal Majesty when he first saw the band perform in the spring of 1997.

Such support would prove invaluable to the band as they established their reputation via the Finnish media. Ville, in particular, benefited greatly from Kallonen's sagacious advice about handling interviews. 'Ville had done some TV and radio interviews with poor results. He didn't bother to answer aloud and he didn't even look where the mike was,' recalled Asko. 'You couldn't hear anything what he was saying. We went to a bar and bought drinks and sat down. I suggested that I ask ten of the most stupid questions that you can imagine and he had to answer them in a very suitable way, look into eyes and speak good Finnish.' After a testing question and answer session with his publicity guru, Ville appeared on Finnish radio the following morning with far greater confidence than had previously been evident.

With the trappings of a soon-to-be-successful group developing around them, their was little need for the band to continue with their day jobs. Linde quit working as an assistant at his father's computer firm. 'It just wasn't my thing,' he observed. Mige also stopped working as an occasional builder and gardener to concentrate on the band. For his part, it was unlikely that Ville would ever want to go back to selling dildos.

> *Sometimes I wish that we'd picked another name for the band than HIM. The name constantly pisses me off. It's utterly terrible. – Ville Valo*

Similarly, Antto had no reason to fall back on his chef's training, as he was inducted into the group as a full member in early 1997. He made his live debut at the Lepakko on 16 May.

The band spent much of the first half of the year writing and rehearsing in preparation for their debut album, which had already been tentatively scheduled for the fall. However, after a further pair of small shows in Helsinki during May, His Infernal Majesty dipped their collective toes in the waters of the festival scene with an appearance at the annual Nummirock heavy metal festival, headlined by mainstream metal behemoths Megadeth also featuring major bands such as Bad Religion alongside Finnish groups like Kyyria and the Rasmus. The band played a twelve-song set that showcased already popular songs such as 'Wicked Game' and 'The Heartless', alongside new material like 'Join Me In Death' and 'Razorblade Kiss' that would later show up on the band's second album. The set finished with a triumphant version of Billy Idol's blockbuster 1984 hit 'Rebel Yell'.

Shortly after this gig, Ville, who has little time for organised religion of any type, realised that the satanic associations implied by the name 'His Infernal Majesty' were inappropriate to the group. 'The name "His Infernal Majesty" was intended as a joke,' he explained. 'But people thought – because of our name and the fact that we're from Scandinavia, that we were Satan worshippers! And that, of course, attracted totally the wrong crowd.'

It was decided to abbreviate the name to HIM, on the basis that it has none of those specific associations, and is short and simple to pronounce in any language. In addition to demonstrating the way in which the group were considering their career at this early stage, the name change also served to free them from being

From sex shop to sex symbol – Ville in winsome mode after the band's first sold-out Tavastia Club gig.

identified with any particular musical genre. This allowed them to explore the entire breadth of their musical influences without being pigeonholed by expectations of conforming to a certain style. 'Early on in Finland we were considered to be pretty satanic, which I disputed in the press,' Ville told *Kerrang!*'s Catherine Yates. 'So all these black metal kids bought tickets to our gigs just to stand at the front wearing corpse paint and spitting on us. It's like, what the fuck are you doing? Spend your £10 on something else – like flowers for mummy.

> *I don't eat meat on tour, because it is too heavy. I wouldn't be able to move my hips on stage if I'd eat those heavy foods. – Ville Valo*

The band made their first official appearance as HIM at the Ilosaarirock festival, which took place at Joensuu, near the Finnish/Russian border. The festival was attended by some 16,000 people and with the band reprising much of their set from a month before, served to further raise their domestic profile.

As the quintet received another good reception at the Ankkarock festival, which took place in Vantaa, just south of Helsinki, it was clear that HIM were arriving. Now all they needed to do was deliver an album that would justify the already burgeoning expectations.

Ville spreads the band's non-satanic message, as Linde fine tunes his amps.

3 in LOVE with DEATH

Elvis is sort of like a Jesus figure to a certain extent . A guy who had it all and fucked it all up. – Ville Valo

Aside from a quartet of concerts within a comfortable day's travel of their Helsinki base during August, HIM spent much of the summer preparing and rehearsing material for their debut album. 'We were totally psyched to have the opportunity to record an album. We didn't know anything about studio technology,' Ville told *Metal Hammer*. 'I was sort of like lyrically waiting for something to happen and always really desperate.'

This desperation was largely due to the paucity of material that Ville felt was good enough for their debut album which simply had to be perfect. Including new versions of 'Wicked Game' and 'The Heartless' the band only had eight songs that they considered suitable for release. The guitar and drum parts were laid down in the MD Studio, which is part of the Munkkiniemi youth centre in Helsinki. The vocals, keyboards and effects were recorded shortly afterwards, either at the Peacemakers Studio in Tuusula, just to the north of Helsinki, or at Finnvox. 'The playing parts were clear when we went to the studio,' Ville explained to the band's Finnish biographer, J. K. Juntenen, 'but anything extra we had to work out with Hiili.'

As with their debut EP, producer Hiili Hiilesmaa played an invaluable role in guiding the inexperienced quintet through the labyrinthine technicalities of the recording process. Described by Ville as 'the sixth member of HIM', Hiilesmaa pieced together the various song elements at the mixing desk to produce a unified whole that matched the band's ideas of how the completed tracks should sound.

Despite his often expressed incredulity at his status, Ville has become established as heavy metal's first genuinely good-looking pin-up.

However, once the eight tracks had been mixed it was felt that at just over 32 minutes, the album was too short. In order to rectify this, HIM recorded a seven minute version of US hard rock combo Blue Oyster Cult's 1976 hit '(Don't Fear) The Reaper'. Ville chose the song because he liked the 'love and death symbolism' that informs much of his own lyrics. 'I got the idea when I was watching the movie *Halloween*,' Ville told Polish radio. 'There was a scene where one of the characters was having a joint in his car and "(Don't Fear) The Reaper" came on the air. I thought, "This is a really great song."' He recorded the vocals as a duet with Sanna-June Hyde, who had previously supplied the filling-loosening scream which can be heard at the beginning of the *666 Ways To Love* version of 'The Heartless'. An 'old crush' of Ville's from elementary school, Sanna-June had recently broken up with Linde, who she had been with for around six years. She would also provide additional vocals to the 1999 version of 'Dark Sekret Love', before going on to establish herself as an actress on Finnish TV. Once '(Don't Fear) The Reaper' was in the can, the album clocked in at around the 40-minute mark, which the group considered to be long enough.

All of a sudden, this nice little hobby started becoming a bit more serious. – Ville Valo

In all, the recording process took fifteen days, with Hiili's mixing taking just a week, after which the tapes were handed over to one of Finnvox's in-house engineers, Pauli Saastamoinen, for mastering. Once this was completed it was decided to trail the album with a single release of 'When Love And Death Embrace', which was issued in Finland on 6 October 1997 as a two-track CD comprising the album version and a radio edit of the song.

'When Love And Death Embrace' sets out both Ville's Byronic lyrical manifesto and HIM's splicing of heavy metal to a melodic pop sensibility with assuredness and clarity. A miasma of emotion and regret, the song is a bittersweet evocation of lost love, driven thunderously on by Linde's churning guitar and given genuine resonance by Ville's demonstration of his vocal range: from reflective baritone to anxious falsetto, all in a little over six minutes. The lyrics are 'like much of Ville's subsequent writing' cleverly constructed, in that their inherent ambiguity makes the song almost universally accessible. Ville, like the overwhelming majority of his early audiences, learned English as a second language. This, to an extent, has informed his songwriting in such a way that precise understanding of every word is unnecessary as the broad meaning of his lyrics is supported by his vocalisations and the group's musical arrangements. 'I learned my English from television. Language is always very visual for me and very musical as well,' Ville told *Modernfix* magazine's Erin

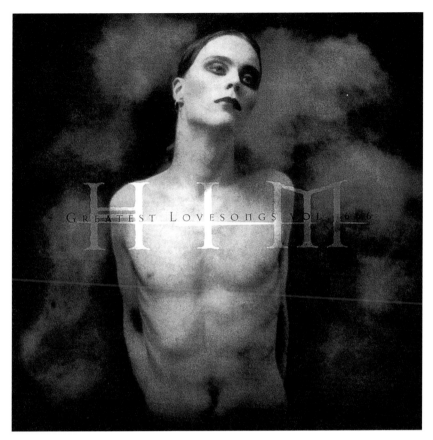

Broadley. 'When I was a bit younger I tried to write in Finnish as well but when a language is so deep inside of you it's hard to get rid of all the clichés. It's easier to play around with the words when you're not speaking them everyday.'

Like the *666 Ways To Love* EP, which was propelled by 'Wicked Game', 'When Love And Death Embrace' peaked in ninth spot on the Finnish singles chart. This was an encouraging response for the band, as it showed that the public were as receptive to their original material as they had been to a song that was already well known on account of Chris Issak's original version, and the exposure it received on the *Wild At Heart* soundtrack.

To promote both the single and forthcoming album, HIM returned to live action, first with a warm-up gig at Tampere's I-Klubi on 18 October, followed by a major support slot six days later backing up Essex techno terrorists the Prodigy at the Hartwall Arena, a newly built all purpose venue that can hold in excess of 12,000 people for concerts. The concert was HIM's first experience of playing such a venue and their set received a muted response from a crowd gathering to see a headline act who shared little musical common ground with Ville and company. Two smaller shows, on their home turf at the Tavastia on 7 November and in the picturesque Eastern town of Kuhmo the following week, saw the band greeted with far greater enthusiasm. Ville was particularly delighted that HIM had succeeded in selling out the Tavastia. 'We would have been very happy with a half filled club, but the club was totally filled. And that's very rare for a Finnish band.'

Happy songs make me very sad. The worst are Vengaboys – I really get depressed. – Ville Valo

Greatest Lovesongs 666 was released across Scandinavia on 20 November 1997. The album opens with 'Your Sweet Six Six Six', a track which, like 'When Love And Death Embrace' serves to introduce the band by laying out their stylistic palate. In this instance, the 'Six six six' motif is used as a lyrical metaphor for the dangers of love, rather than the promotion of Satanism. As Ville was at pains to point out, 'We have nothing to do with Satan.' This non-satanic usage is reinforced by the album art, which includes the number of the beast placed within a heart to indicate the relationship between love and ultimate destruction. 'Does only Satan have sole rights to death?' asked Ville. 'Love is about small deaths all the time. 666 indicates love's more carnal and fixational aspects.'

Musically, the band again tempers their Black Sabbath influences with a mainstream, eighties influenced pop sensibility – a mixture of heavy and light, which Ville identifies as a key element in the group's sound: 'It's a perfect link: two things that are something completely different, but fit each other, like Chinese signs yin and yang. Besides, we've got more things in common with a guy like Chris Isaak than with any metallic band full of testosterone.' This juxtaposition is particularly apparent toward the end of the track, when Ville's whispered vocal during the bridge section crashes out into the anthemic chorus.

After reworked versions of 'Wicked Game' and 'The Heartless' – the latter emerging as poppier and far more texturally rich than the heavier version to be found on the *His Infernal Majesty* EP – HIM demonstrate their dexterity across the opus of 'Our Diabolikal Rapture'. Co-written by Linde, the song is a churning, flange-driven paen to the single-minded totality of love. The complex arrangement was such that the band found it difficult to reproduce the song live.

'It's All Tears (Drown In This Love)' finds Ville again casting himself in the role of diabolical lover promising to 'violate you in the most sensual way'. Vocally, he delivers the song as a duet, shared between his deep baritone lead and impassioned high register counterpoint set atop perhaps the most straightforward metal arrangement on the album. 'When Love And Death Embrace' provides an oasis of reflective melancholy ahead of the morbid apocalyptica of 'The Beginning Of The End'. Again combining elements that would not sound out of place on a Metallica album with a fragile description of doomed love, the song impressively demonstrates the band's range and still remains on many HIM fans' favourites lists. Reflecting upon the way in which his wide variety of influences were applied to the album, Ville observed, 'There hasn't been one scene for me – I was always into good songs. I like songs by the Eurythmics, but also from Dimmu Borgir. Maybe that's the reason why HIM's music is so different.'

The group's grandiose interpretation of '(Don't Fear) The Reaper' appropriately sets up the album's valedictory track, set opener 'For You'. Described by Ville as 'my hymn', the song is a tender yet heavy declaration of immortal love. 'My songs are always about relationships or women', he explained. 'I just can't write about anything else.'

The album's running time is extended to 66:06 by the inclusion of a series of silent (aside from a short instrumental section taken from the EP version of 'The Heartless') tracks. Ville subsequently told German magazine *Bravo* this was little more than a numerological jest. 'The point to the hidden song was that we wanted to make the duration of the record 66 minutes and 6 seconds. We had to have enough sixes, there's nothing more into it. Bad humour, that's all.'

When we're touring in America we'll crack up. Then we will be real rockstars and only give interviews for cash. – Mige Amour

Greatest Lovesongs 666 received what Ville described as 'tiny recognition by the Finnish and European press' and climbed to Number 4 on the Finnish chart. With a domestic tour lined up for December, the band sought Seppo Vesterinen's counsel. 'Their first album was out in Finland and they had generated a measure of interest in other countries; there were also quite a few publishers who wanted them to sign a publishing deal,' he explained. 'They wanted advice on those aspects, and that's how we started. We decided not to sign publishing to anyone.'

Following a well-received eight-date Finnish tour, which started with a short 'greatest hits' set at the Tavastia on 5 December and ended back in Helsinki with a show at the Lepakko club on New Year's Eve, HIM invited Seppo to manage them. He readily agreed. not only did he like the band and their music, but also saw in them 'a potential for growth and for long-term careers'.

For the five members of HIM, 1998 was the year that music became the day job. Beginning in the central Finnish town of Siilinjärvi on 9 January, the quintet would play almost 80 shows in their most sustained bout of touring to date. The first half of the year saw the band criss-cross the country relentlessly, honing their stage act and gathering new fans in the process. On 7 February they played an all-ages show at the Road House in Hämeenlinna, which lies some 30 miles south-east of Tampere. This was the first of a number of such concerts HIM would play and clearly demonstrated the appeal of the band to the younger Finnish audience, as well as the older, more committed gig-goers who turned up in increasing numbers at their shows.

Five days earlier, BMG Finland issued the second single to be drawn from *Greatest Lovesongs 666* – 'Your Sweet Six Six Six', which was backed with two remixes of 'The Beginning Of The End': the electronica-influenced 'Tandeberg B74 mix' and the thunderous 'Satanik Love Mix'. These two remixes served to make this edition of the single hugely collectable among fans and the Finnish only release rose to Number 7 on the domestic chart.

After a three week break in early February, the band returned to the road playing small clubs throughout March, April and May – their country-wide sorties being interspersed with shows in Helsinki, usually at the Tavastia or Lepakko. The summer months saw the band embracing the festival circuit to a far greater extent than the previous year. Starting with an appearance at Helsinki's annual free Puistorock event at the end of May, HIM appeared at all of Finland's major outdoor festivals and made their debut outside of their homeland with an appearance alongside rock heavyweights such as Rage Against The Machine and Rammstein at Sweden's annual multi-stage Hultsfred pop, rock and metal festival.

Throughout the summer, HIM expanded their fanbase on an almost daily basis, with much of the band's early press focusing on Ville and remarking on his resemblance to the legendary Doors frontman, Jim Morrison. For his part, Ville couldn't see the likeness. 'I never understood that,' he told *Metal Hammer*. 'Someone compares me with Jim Morrison just because I have curls and a similar hair colour.' Seen live, Ville's louche stage presence, languid vocal style and omnipresent bottle of wine only served to draw further comparisons with the Lizard King. As HIM's public face, Ville would find himself compared to everyone from Syd Barrett to Frank Sinatra. This didn't bother the vocalist over-much. 'I don't mind being compared to legends,' he observed.

Ville's penchant for hanging on to a bottle of wine and chain-smoking through performances had more to do with overcoming stage fright than any affected evocation of past heroes. 'When I was a bassist and a guitarist, I used to have something in my hands,' he explained. 'Then when I had my first gig as a singer, I didn't know what to do with my hands.' Although Ville opted to drink wine rather than beer onstage, as the bubbles in beer made him burp, he soon abandoned the practice as he found it was having an adverse effect on his voice.

As HIM's public profile rose so did their marketability, and the band signed a licensing deal with BMG Germany, which saw 'Wicked Game' re-issued in Germany and *Greatest Lovesongs 666* get its European release. This single hit German shelves on 28 September and was supported by the band's first professionally shot promotional video. Directed by Marcus Walter, who would subsequently go on to make promos for bands such as electronica duo Zero 7 and English indie band Reef, the

The less sex I have, the more inspiration I have for beautiful songs. – Ville Valo

promo pitches the band into a snow globe electric ladyland filled with gothic ruins and PVC clad dark angels. Unfortunately for Antto, Walter was labouring under the misapprehension that the band were a quartet and shot the bulk of the footage without the keyboard player. Once the error was realised, Antto was dressed as a snowman for a brief clip that appears right at the very end of the video.

Antto's non-appearance in the video was soon mirrored by his status within the band. As HIM wound their way around Finland it became apparent that while Ville was fiercely driven to making the group a success, Antto was significantly more laid back. This was viewed by Ville as laziness, and the differences in the two bandmates' personalities quickly developed into a full-blown conflict, exacerbated by the claustrophobic atmosphere that comes with being on tour. This was affecting the atmosphere within HIM and after a final gig at the Helsinki Arts Festival on 22 August, Antto left the band and returned to working as a chef.

His replacement was not long in coming. At the recommendation of Pätkä, the band asked Jussi-Miko Salminen to take over from Antto. Known to his friends as Juska, the twenty-year-old keyboard player had recently recorded an EP as part of Kouvola-based glam rockers Mary Ann, who had morphed into a new outfit called To/Die/For shortly before Juska was invited to join HIM. Although his musical interests were primarily based around techno and other electronic genres, Juska was also an admirer of HIM and had been hugely impressed by *Greatest Lovesongs 666*. His reaction on being asked to join was to pay a swift visit to the bathroom to throw up.

Initially, Juska found adapting to life in HIM a little difficult. His musical tastes were very different from those of his new bandmates and he found it difficult to grasp rock and metal based reference points that Ville, Linde, Mige and Pätkä were completely familiar with. Additionally, with the band's first tour of Germany looming, there was some question as to whether Juska would be ready in time, and it was suggested that Antto might rejoin for these dates. After a brief period of uncertainty during September, Juska was taken through the HIM song catalogue by Ville and underwent a series of highly productive rehearsals with the rest of the band. By the following month he was passed ready to join the band on tour and assumed the suitably rock stage name of Zoltan Pluto.

With *Greatest Lovesongs 666* tickling the bottom end of the German Top 50, and the 'Wicked Game' re-issue (which also included 'For You', 'Our Diabolikal Rapture' and a coruscating '666 Remix' of the title track) serving as an introduction to the band for German audiences, HIM were set for their first foreign tour.

Juska made his debut on 28 November at the first of HIM's week of club gigs throughout Germany. After an appearance on the *Viva Overdrive* TV show – which was shot in Cologne on 7 December – band and road crew travelled to Austria for a pair of shows in Vienna and Linz, before completing their tour with a quartet of concerts in Switzerland. After Christmas, the HIM New Year's Eve tradition was maintained as they returned to Austria for a performance at Soul City in Vienna.

Although Juska was bedding in nicely, there were problems behind the drum kit. With sessions already underway to work up new material for the follow-up to *Greatest Lovesongs 666*, Pätkä was finding it difficult to commit to the band. '[He] only wanted to rehearse once or twice a month,' explained Ville. 'So we had no chance to develop.' The roots of Pätkä's dilemma lay in his girlfriend becoming pregnant and his increasingly heavy drinking, which served to make him somewhat unre-

HIM snuggle up for a publicity shot – the tattoo on Ville's left arm took several hours to complete and, despite the numbing effects of alcohol, proved a painful ordeal.

liable. With HIM committed to a second German tour in March and April and with record company pressure to deliver the second album increasing, the group could not accommodate a part-time drummer. And so Pätkä left the band.

Some less than successful attempts to record new songs using a drum machine and the approaching German dates underlined the necessity of finding a replacement for Pätkä. As a temporary solution, Ville got in touch with former Kyyria drummer Gas

Above: Gas examines Migé's credentials.

Lipstick, who had been working as a drum technician with Finnish power metal legends Stratovarius. 'I got a phone call from Ville,' explains Gas. 'He told me that they've parted company with their drummer and needed someone to step in and do the remaining German tour dates. I thought, "What the hell, why not?" I didn't have a band at the time, because we had split up with Kyyria a couple of months earlier.'

The timing couldn't have been better for Gas, who was considering relocating to Stockholm, London or Los Angeles, in search of a band in need of a drummer. Having spent seven years in Kyyria, he was reluctant to start from scratch with a new group, and thus more than happy to accept Ville's offer.

We are the negative version of Bon Jovi. The bad thing is good and the good thing is bad. – Ville Valo

Born Mika Kristian Karppinen in the Swedish industrial city of Eskilstuna on 8 February 1971, Gas was the only child of Finnish migrants who had moved to Sweden in search of work. Both his parents were musically inclined – his father, who worked at the Volvo car manufacturing plant, used to play the accordion, while his mother had a good voice and took great pleasure in singing. As an infant, Gas was constantly banging out rhythms on pots, pans and whatever else he could get his inquisitive hands on. To encourage his development, his parents bought him a toy guitar, drum set and piano as Christmas presents when he was three years old. His father played in a local accordion ensemble and Gas regularly tagged along. 'I really loved the sound of the drums and got interested in the instrument,' he recalled. 'I remember asking the drummer if he would let me play his drum kit. And he was kind enough to let me do that. So during the next practice I was counting seconds and waiting for the break. He later on became my first drum teacher.'

At the age of six, Gas discovered heavy metal through his friend Harri Mänty's big brother, who was a huge Kiss fan. At kindergarten, Gas, Harri (who went on to play guitar in Swedish indie pop giants Kent) and chums got made up as the band and mimed to their songs: 'I remember me being Gene Simmons and Harri, Paul Stanley – that made me realise I wanted to be a musician.' As he entered adolescence, Gas' tastes began shifting toward the extreme end of the rock spectrum, with bands such as Slayer and English anarcho-punks Discharge becoming his all-time favourites. When he was eleven years old, he formed his first band with Harri and some local friends – the delightfully named Hairless Future.

In 1984, the Karpinnen family returned to Finland and although he was initially reluctant to leave his friends back in Eskilstuna – taking around eighteen months to settle into his new surroundings – Gas applied himself to honing his guitar and drum skills. During his first summer in Finland, his father sent him to a music camp where he met some other attendees who had an interest in thrash and hardcore punk. They formed a band called Valvontakomissio, which would endure for over six years, with Gas swapping guitar for drums and vocals along the way. 'My dad always told me that I sounded like a wounded pig,' laughed Gas.

Valvontakomissio gigged regularly and built up a local reputation, travelling as far as Jakutsk in Siberia to play at the town's Peace & Love festival. The band recorded a number of demos and in 1991 contributed fourteen tracks to a split album they shared with another local hardcore outfit, No Security. A further seventeen tracks were released on *Systeemi Tappaa* (Kill The System) in 1994. The CD sleeve is a faithful recreation of that found on Discharge's *Realities Of War* EP, further underlining the influence of the proto-thrash quartet on Gas' music. Indeed, in 1991 Gas even went so far as to play bass in a side project that went by the name of Dischange, whose brief blasts of sonic fury and anarchistic lyrics could almost have been cloned from the band to which they paid such evident homage.

In 1992, Gas joined Kyyria as drummer. He describes this period as 'the most educational of my early musical career,' and played with the alt-metal outfit on two EP's and an album, *Blessed Ravings*, which were released in Finland, Germany and France during 1994-95. The group also toured both at home and abroad, and it was whilst in Kyyria that Gas assumed his remarkable name. 'We had an idea about forming a glam rock band,' he explained. 'At a party we came up with the most ridiculous artist names and "Gas Lipstick" sounded so funny that I decided to use it on a Kyyria record. Somehow I've ended up dragging that name along with me.'

Metal isn't macho. It's asexual – like Gas...
– Emerson Burton

Whilst with Kyyria, Gas also found time to provide guitar and vocals for another band, speed metal outfit Dementia, who released an eponymous nine track album in 1995.

Gas made his debut as stand-in drummer on the opening night of HIM's second German tour on 30 March 1999. Although he recalls being 'really nervous' before the show at the Soundgarden Club in Dortmund, the gig went well and his extensive reservoir of experience helped him to settle into the band without any great difficulty. On 10 April, during the final concert of HIM's eleven-date tour, Ville made an announcement to the audience at Munich's Backstage Club: 'We have a new drummer in the band – his name is Gas Lipstick.' This confirmed Gas' full time membership of the group, 'A special moment,' beamed Gas.

In addition to the successful assimilation of Gas into the group and the positive reception from the German audiences, Ville had his first experience of overzealous fan worship after the Hamburg show on 4 April. 'He was enjoying his drink in the bar,' recounted Gas, 'and suddenly this crazy, totally wasted Polish girl storms in with a pair of scissors in her hand. She cuts a piece from his hair and starts to laugh hysterically.'

Lunatic fans notwithstanding, HIM returned to Germany for a trio of major open air engagements in late May. They appeared at the massive Rock am Ring Festival at the Nürnbergring racetrack, as well as its twin event the Rock im Park event and the Wave Gothic festival, which took place in Leipzig. The band made several further festival appearances in Germany, Austria, Switzerland and Finland during the summer, but by early September the group stopped gigging in order to finally record definitive versions of the songs that were to make up their second album.

> *Once when I was about ten, I stole a chocolate bar. I was a really nice kid. I probably tried it out to see what it felt like. – Gas Lipstick*

Three months earlier, Ville had met up with British based producer John Fryer who had previously worked with bands such as Nine Inch Nails, White Zombie and Fear Factory. He invited the band over to record some demos at Rockfield Studios in Wales and although Ville was initially worried that the band's songs might be drowned in production and samples, the band made a whistlestop visit to the Principality and laid down three tracks. 'We thought that John Fryer would tell us exactly what we are supposed to do – that he won't be fair to us, but it wasn't like that at all,' explained Ville. The band were so impressed with both the producer and his work that they returned to Rockfield in September 1999 in order to complete the album.

During the album sessions Ville was contacted by BMG, who asked him if he had heard of the forthcoming film adaptation of Daniel F. Galouye's novel *The Thirteenth Floor*. It transpired that there was a possibility of the band submitting a song for inclusion on the soundtrack. 'At first I was a bit sceptical,' confessed Ville. 'But after they had sent me a copy of the movie and gave me some background information I thought it was great.'

However, with the band in the midst of recording at Rockwell, there was no time to record an exclusive song for the soundtrack. Instead, the band submitted 'Join Me In Death', one of the three tracks that had been initially recorded during their early summer visit to the studio and was therefore in an advanced state of readiness. The response from the makers of *The Thirteenth Floor* was hugely enthusiastic and the song was earmarked for inclusion on both the soundtrack and its accompanying album.

In order to capitalise on this promotional opportunity it was decided to release the song as a single in both Finland and Germany. Its title shortened to the less controversial 'Join Me', the single came out, complete with a movie tie-in sleeve, on 2 November

Gas Lipstick: Drum leviathan, rock icon, sex god.

1999 and surpassed all expectations by hitting the Number 1 slot in both countries.

A bittersweet evocation of love and fatalism, 'Join Me' showcased Ville's sensitive vocals amid a haze of swirling rock guitar and delicate piano. Again, the vocalist's lyrical use of the death motif, with lines such as 'Won't you die tonight for love' and the 'Join me in death' refrain drew criticism from parents' associations on the basis that they represented an endorsement of suicide. Ville told *Rennbahn Express* magazine that he thought such an interpretation was 'Foolish – "Join Me" is simply a modern version of the classical *Romeo and Juliet* topic.'

'The "Join Me In Death" lyrics were symbolic,' confirmed Mige. 'They became a reason for us to be misunderstood, as many people considered that we suggested suicide. But with "death" we symbolised the end of a relationship, the end of love, we didn't mean physical death.' The single was supported by a video shot by Australian director John Hillcoat, who had previously worked with Nick Cave, the Manic Street Preachers, Siouxsie and the Banshees and Placebo and would subsequently direct Cave's visceral depiction of colonial Australia, *The Proposition* (2005). Like the 'Wicked Game' promo, the video transports HIM to another sub-arctic wonderland, this time populated with blue-lipped ice queens, dramatic frozen palaces and elements of fairytales such as *Snow White* and *Red Riding Hood*. Although 'Wicked Game' was an important song in terms of breaking HIM in Finland and Germany, 'Join Me' would be the point at which many of the band's committed fanbase would discover the group.

I hate talking about my own songs. They're all about women anyway. – Ville Valo

Described by Ville as 'the perfect synthesis of rock songs with pop appeal and melancholic ballads', the remainder of the songs for the forthcoming album were recorded and mixed at Rockfield, Finnvox and London's Strongroom studios in a lightning-fast three week blast of sustained creativity. Ville was enthusiastic about John Fryer's work, crediting the producer with showing the band 'another way to work' and stating that his influence guided them toward a more straightforward, rock-orientated sound stripped of complex samples and overdubs. 'We didn't want to use loads of sequencers, or computerised things, or loops,' asserted Ville. 'We want to be able to reproduce the sound of the album live.'

Originally conceived under the Bon Jovi-referencing title 'Slippery When Dead', *Razorblade Romance* finally saw the light of day on 24 January 2000, with 'Join Me In Death' among eleven tracks, all of which were written by Ville. 'With this album we want to emphasise our own songs more,' he told German magazine *Sonic Seducer*. 'It's a strange feeling "Wicked Game" as been the biggest hit on the last

The face that launched a thousand heartagram tattoos.

1999's Razorblade Romance *was the band's breakthrough album, establishing HIM across Europe.*

album and not one of my own songs. We don't want to be labelled as a metal juke-box which only is successful with compositions of other musicians.'

The album opens with 'I Love You (Prelude To Tragedy)', a pounding statement of romantic fatalism, which benefits from an uncluttered arrangement that sets the intro-spective mood for the remainder of the disc. Like the opener, 'Poison Girl' begins soft-ly before erupting into an emotionally charged recountment of a manipulative relation-ship; the song would later be released as the third single from the album and climb to third spot on the Finnish Chart, supported by a live video which showed Ville stripping off to the moist delight of his audience. After the anthemic 'Join Me In Death', 'Right Here In My Arms' sees the LP take an upbeat tone and features a remarkable effects-laden lead from Linde, and a chorus sufficiently catchy to ensure this song would be selected as the second single from *Razorblade Romance*.

The album's outstanding ballad, 'Gone With The Sin' showcases Ville's intimate vocal style to great effect. As with the use of 'death' in 'Join Me', 'sin' in this instance is used as a metaphor. '"Sin" symbolises the irresolution, the bad behaviour towards him-self – not the sin in the religious sense,' explained Ville. 'I deal with people who don't know what to do with their lives. Who die because of their self-pity and who complain about everything but never have the idea to take charge of their lives themselves.'

The edgy live favourite, 'Razorblade Kiss' provides Linde with another opportunity to rock out with a bravura solo, earning him an extra sleeve credit for his Daniel Lioneye persona. HIM's range is again highlighted by the shift in tone to the next track, the emotionally inundated power ballad, 'Bury Me Deep Inside Your Heart', which sees the band switch from crunching chords to fragile melody, as Ville surrenders his lyrical troth with sensitivity and strength. 'It has a little of a Depeche Mode on a keyboards and Black Sabbath on guitars,' he observed. 'And it's really in the same vein as "Gone With The Sin". It's just a love song.'

The only song not road-tested by the band prior to recording *Razorblade Romance*, 'Heaven Tonight' is an eighties-tinged, liquid bass driven hymn to lust and desire, which finds Ville at his most sultry. The rockier 'Death Is In Love With Us' is notable for being the only point on the album that Ville uses the '666' device so prevalent on *Greatest Lovesongs 666* ('41 plus 66.6 equals our loss'). 'It was so tiring when everyone asked about it. Maybe we will come back to it. But too often it was just misunderstood, it became a burden.'

I'm living my dream right now. I get to make music, perform and travel. – Ville Valo

The album's penultimate track, 'Resurrection' is another number suffused with more traditional rock elements. An intense, escapist description of doomed romance notable for Ville's almost sexual vocalisations, the song highlights the way in which the dynamic musical synthesis within HIM creates an expansive sound in an apparently effortless manner. The disc concludes with 'One Last Time', a heartbreakingly inspirational number that differs from the live rendition of the song, courtesy of Linde's excellent acoustic guitar during the song's opening. Given 'One Last Time''s heartfelt evocation of impending loss, it was a pity that the track was not included on subsequent foreign editions of the album, which saw it supplanted by versions of 'Your Sweet 666' and 'Wicked Game'.

Propelled by the success of 'Join Me', *Razorblade Romance* hit the top of the Finnish and then the German charts. The album would also go on to achieve platinum status and take the Number 1 slot in Austria. To celebrate, BMG held a champagne party. But elsewhere, Ville and Mige were not yet enjoying the fruits of their success. 'We were sitting in a bar with Mige and we were speculating; where do we get the money to buy ourselves a pint of beer to celebrate – it's the record company that gets all the money – we don't get anything,' laughed Ville.

4 I'm YOUR CHRIST

*I would die for love. – **Ville Valo***
Love is my religion, I could die for it.
*– **John Keats***

Following the chart-topping success of *Razorblade Romance*, HIM looked to consolidate their rapidly expanding Finnish and German fanbases by heading out on an extensive spring tour that would also see them revisit Austria and Switzerland, as well as exploring the previously uncharted territories of Holland, Belgium, Luxembourg and the Czech Republic.

This latest mammoth bout of touring kicked off on 18 February 2000 at Club Moo, in the city of Pori, which lies on Finland's western coast and continued almost without a break until the band completed their set at the 5000-capacity Phillipshalle in Dusseldorf on 23 April. Every one of the German concerts was a complete sell-out, with black market tickets commanding premium prices. The crowds directed much of their enthusiasm at Ville, who basked coolly in the waves of rapture, sublimating the oestrogen-rich torrents of desire into the erotic *froideur* of his performance. 'The 23-year-old heartthrob attracts attention without running like mad across the stage,' observed *Bravo* in the German magazine's review of HIM's 26 March Hamburg concert. The rest of the band supplied a solid rock backdrop to Ville's lasciviousness, content to act as a sonic frame within which their frontman increasingly embodied desire.

Initially, Ville was uncertain of how to react to such raw excitement from the band's audiences, and tended to turn away from the crowd as a kind of subconscious defence

Profile of a post-millennial rock icon – Ville perfects his middle-distance stare.

mechanism. 'It's really weird to be put on a pedestal with thousands of people clapping their hands to the song you wrote a year and a half ago sitting on your bed wearing your underwear because you felt so fucking bad,' he told *Modern Fix* magazine's Erin Broadley. 'It's a thing my brain doesn't compute to a certain extent, but I'm getting used to it.' Indeed, Ville's confidence seemed to grow with every passing gig, and by the time the tour was in full swing he was positively enjoying himself. 'Adrenaline is a wonderful thing – and maybe two beers before the gig,' he laughed. 'It feels like one day I'm going to wake up in a room and find out that it's all been an LSD experiment by the Finnish military.'

The rest of the band and crew also had fun on the tour; during his 'Wicked Game' solo, Linde reduced Ville and Mige to fits of giggles by repeatedly slipping over on a slippery spot on the Turbinehalle, Oberhausen stage. 'It was the worst possible moment and I'm sure each and every one in the audience and at least Ville and Mige on stage noticed it because they were laughing their asses off and I was *so* embarrassed,' he recalled. Drum tech Sean McCarthy instigated a ritual of decorating Gas' drums with any underwear that was thrown onto the stage. 'That makes me wonder, because I've noticed his almost hysterical interest in bras and female clothing,' grinned Gas.

Despite the success of the tour, the group were pleased to get home for a couple of weeks at the end of April 2000. 'After the tour in the spring we were completely bushed,' recalled Ville. 'But some free days at home in Helsinki brought back our consumed energy.' After the hysteria of the German concerts, returning to friends and family represented a welcome re-entry to planet earth. 'They don't treat us like stars here, they treat us like they treat usual people,' Ville explained. 'When we are in Helsinki for a short time, we all sleep at our parents' homes. Although everyone has got their own small flats, we like being with our family – you don't have to care about anything at Mama's home.'

While HIM were on tour, 'Right Here In My Arms' was released as a single in both Finland and Germany. The single was accompanied by a promotional video shot by Finnish director Pasi Pauni who had previously worked with Apocalyptica and Ultra Bra. The film sees HIM rock out behind wired glass, as if to underline the barrier between artist and audience. The performance is imbued with further post-modern awareness by a disinterested-yet-playful Ville. Live, the song was a popular set opener that exemplified the group's effortlessly broad grandeur and would often see Ville adopting mock-ironic 'rock' attitudes as he pouted and strutted through the song. The single was released in two formats in both countries, hitting the Number 1 spot in Finland and managing Number 22 in Germany. The German edition featured new mixes of 'Join Me In Death' and 'The Heartless', in addition to a new track, 'I've Crossed Oceans Of Wine To Find You', a Hammond organ-driven torch song based on Vlad Tepes' line from the film *Bram Stoker's Dracula*: 'I've crossed oceans of time to find you.' The song itself was actually a demo version of 'Resurrection' that

We are like chameleons, we can be whatever we want to be. If one day we decide to get really drunk we can paint our faces and pretend that we are Michael Jackson. – Ville Valo

predated *Razorblade Romance*.

As HIM's profile increased with each successive gig or record release, so did European press interest in the band. Many journalists, groping to encapsulate the *gestalt* of influences which had coalesced into the band's sound, reached for the nearest genre and identified HIM as a goth ensemble. This pigeonholing was exacerbated by record company press releases which identified the group and their music as 'goth'n'roll'.

My goal is to get a job on a ferry sailing between Helsinki and Stockholm and sing tangos. – Ville Valo

However, Ville was dismissive of such a narrow definition of the band. 'We've got nothing to do with the gothic scene,' he told *Sonic Seducer*. 'Of course this genre does have certain influences on the lyrics. But we're much more: we are metal, gothic, pop – a 666 piece jigsaw puzzle.' This was a fair assertion, as HIM's music and image transcended the parameters of what's customarily defined as gothic in a pop cultural sense. The accessibility and universal nature of the group's material runs counter to a scene that is inherently exclusive, wilfully separate from the mainstream. 'I think that we are a special shade of goth,' mused Ville in an interview with Greek magazine *Pop & Rock*. 'We are tenderer than others of that kind of music. This obsession with gothic has more to do with my other personal tastes – I liked being dressed in black clothes – but also with the Finnish musical tradition. Our traditional music is very melancholic.'

In order to demonstrate their detachment from the overtly gothic, the sleeve art to *Razorblade Romance* steered well clear of any crepuscular symbolism, presenting Ville as an androgynous glam icon, making prominent use of a bright pink colour scheme and the vocalist's smouldering sexuality. 'I wanted to get away from this visual gothic image,' he revealed. 'Dark colours and gloomy figures – all these things don't fascinate me anymore. I'm taking the liberty to change like I want to. And by the way – I'm still heterosexual.'

With BMG now promoting HIM throughout Europe and the twelve-track version of *Razorblade Romance*, the band set off to make a live impression on hitherto unexplored territories. Beginning in Porto at the Parque da Cidade on 11 May 2000, the quintet played six shows in Portugal. This was followed by a UK debut at London's Garage on 19 May, then a further five dates in England and Scotland, a trio of dates in Spain and a one off appearance in Bonn, Germany on 3 June. During July, Ville found time to perform a couple of sets of Raul Badding Somerjoki's material at the Teerenpeli bar in the city of Lahti, which lies on the southern edge of the Vesijärvi lake, about 60 miles north of Helsinki. The same month saw the single release of

Above and right: Away from the relentless grind of touring and recording, Ville takes time to chill out amid the verdant splendour of the Finnish countryside.

'Poison Girl', which was issued with live versions of 'Right Here In My Arms' and 'It's All Tears'. The single hit the Number 3 slot in Finland and made the German Top 40.

In keeping with previous years, the summer brought HIM into the daylight as they embraced the festival season as never before, appearing at around twenty festivals in more than a dozen countries. Perhaps the most memorable of the band's outdoor shows was their appearance at the Highfield Festival in the east German city of Erfurt on 20 August. HIM were caught in a torrential downpour, which ultimately caused them to abandon their set. 'We played three songs and suddenly it rained cats and dogs,' Ville told *Orkus* magazine. 'The water was ten centimetres high on stage. Everybody was completely wet, and the people started to throw mud on stage. Finally we had to break off the gig – the equipment on stage was ruined, the PA broke down. Nothing worked.'

Keen not to let down their disappointed fans, HIM scheduled a show at Erfurt's Messhalle for 24 September 2000 where anyone with a ticket from the washed-out festival was allowed in for free.

Despite their hectic touring schedule and the continued chart successes of their singles, HIM were already thinking about a third studio album. Taking some time out during August to demo material for an album conceived under the working title of *Ozymandius Dargunum*, the band prepared fourteen songs at the Petrax studio in Hollola, near Lahti. 'I imagine it will be more melodic, more seventies – something like Led Zeppelin,' Ville revealed. 'With our first album we were in the nineties, with the second the eighties and with the third the seventies – we have to follow our tradition that inverts the decades.'

However, the band's hectic schedule left little opportunity to work up the new material, and work on the new album was set aside until the following year. To maintain HIM's chart profile, on 23 October 2000 BMG issued a fourth single from *Razorblade Romance* – 'Gone With The Sin'. Helped by a pastoral psychedelic promo shot by Bill Yükich (who had previously directed videos by Marilyn Manson, Metallica and Courtney Love's Hole, as well as a stack of R&B product) the single became the band's third Finnish Number 1 and reached Number 19 in Germany. The single featured an orchestral version of 'Gone With The Sin' arranged by respected composer and jazz trumpeter Otto Donner, described by the Finnish Music Information Centre as 'the Miles Davis of the Arctic region'.

Further releases followed during November with 'Wicked Game' hitting the shelves in Holland and Taiwan. In addition to widening their international profile through further dates in England, Greece, Spain, France, Italy, Slovenia, Holland, Poland, Belgium, Latvia and Estonia, the autumn saw HIM receive a steady trickle of awards. Finnish radio station Radiomafia (who had helped arrange the collaboration with Otto Donner) held a poll which resulted in Ville being voted as the nation's most stylish pop performer. In Germany, where *Razorblade Romance* had just gone platinum, music channel Viva presented the band with an award for the most requested videos

Lost in music – Ville gives it his all in the studio.

and the state television station ZDF handed the group their 'most desired band' prize. Seppo Vesterinen was also named as the Finnish manager of the year, and the band even received the backhanded compliment of being parodied by Eläkeläiset (Finnish for 'pensioners'), a popular folk/comedy ensemble who had previously worked their riotous accordion driven magic on *humppa* versions of Iron Maiden's 'Run To The Hills', Nirvana's 'Smells Like Teen Spirit' and Bon Jovi's 'Livin' On A Prayer'.

Ville was sanguine about the band's success. 'There is no change for me,' he remarked. 'We just notice our shows take place in bigger venues . . . and that more people want to hear our songs and that they also know the lyrics and that the number of lighters at the melancholic songs has risen. But that's all.'

However, unlike his frontman, Zoltan was not taking HIM's success in his stride. For him, success equated with pressure. He suffered from a lack of confidence in his musical ability and felt that he might be letting the group down in some way. The keyboardist also found that appearing on television and doing interviews was not to his liking. 'I was too tired,' he told *Rennbahn Express* in 2001. 'All the noise around our band was too much for me.'

Zoltan discussed his feelings with the band, his father and other friends before deciding to leave HIM. 'We always understood each other very well and we are still good friends, but they accepted my decision.' After fulfilling his responsibilities on the band's five-date December 2000 tour of Portugal, Zoltan made his farewell appearance at HIM's now-customary New Year's Eve show at the Tavastia Club. Subsequently, Zoltan confessed to some regrets about making his decision so quickly. 'I'm sad – a nice relationship came to an end and I'm missing our time together. I'm sorry that I don't belong to them anymore.'

With only a small number of dates lined up for the beginning of 2001, Zoltan's departure was timed with some consideration for his bandmates – allowing them ample time before the next bout of serious touring and recognising the fact that Ville would be more than capable of playing keyboards on the forthcoming album sessions.

To bring the band up to full strength for a short run of four shows across Scandinavia during January, they once again called upon Burton who had last played with HIM just over five years earlier. He had since been gigging with goth rockers Sub-Urban Tribe and Torpedo, with whom he had recently recorded a thirteen-track album *Polttonestettä*, due for release by Ranka Recordings in March 2001. Burton had a long association with the group, particularly Mige whom he had been at school with, and was pleased to see them enjoying a good deal of success. 'It was funny and interesting to see the band's evolution in the newspapers and all this stuff. And, of course, I was happy because they made it.'

Burton made his second debut as a temporary member of the band at a hastily arranged concert at the SemiFinal Club on 12 January 2001. The show was set up in order to give the keyboard player the chance to appear live in a low-key environ-

Usually I'm the one to blame, you know,
I'm the one that has to carry the burden about
making decisions. – Ville Valo

ment, ahead of the dates in Sweden, Norway and Denmark later in the month. Burton found that playing with HIM was 'really easy and comfortable', a feeling that was reciprocated by his new bandmates, who had been more than happy to help him learn the set. It was a natural progression when he was asked to become a full-time member at the end of January.

Although much of the material for the third album had been recorded, a series of production issues had ensured that neither band nor record company was particularly pleased with the results. The basic tracks had been recorded with Finnish engineer Timo Tapani Oksala, after which former Aerosmith and Iron Maiden producer Kevin 'the Caveman' Shirley was flown in to complete the album. 'We'd got into Fu Manchu and all those stoner type bands and recorded a demo, which we wanted to be the album, which the record label didn't like at all,' explained Ville. 'We ended up fighting about it, building the album on top of demos with different producers. Our keyboard player left so I played some of the keyboards on the album. Burton also came and played. It was just a big hassle; it took a whole eleven months to finish that particular record.'

We needed to do something totally different and that's when Daniel Lioneye happened. – *Ville Valo*

To add to the creative problems, the record company employed a variety of technicians at the mixing stage, which led to further disagreements as to which versions of what songs should be included on the finished disc. 'It created a lot of hassle and a lot of speculation,' Ville told Belgian radio's Tom Aerts. 'When you have around 30 to 40 songs all mixed four times by different people, and a couple of remixes of several tracks . . . instead of having something like thirteen good tracks you have tens and tens of tracks to choose from. And that's a waste of time.'

While Ville worked with the production engineers on the mixing at Finnvox, the rest of the band took a break and did some travelling, with Gas heading for New York, while Mige and Linde went to Jamaica. Finally, the album was sent to the US for another mixing session that involved both Kevin Shirley and John Fryer. With some time on their hands, Linde, Mige and Ville began working on a side project under the name of Daniel Lioneye, that would ultimately result in *The King Of Rock'n Roll* album.

Daniel Lioneye had its roots in quiet periods during HIM sessions, which involved Linde taking over vocal duties from Ville, while the frontman played drums. 'After some HIM rehearsals me, Mige and Ville just started to jam on my catchy and groovy stoner riffs and realised that we are an excellent trio. We used to practise once a year and in two years time we were ready to go to the studio.' In keeping with the fun nature of the project the trio adopted new personas within the group; Linde became 'Daniel Lioneye' ('my funny Rastafarian name that we invented when we were sitting

The King of Rock'n Roll - *The debut album from the Linde-led side-project, Daniel Lioneye featured new personas for Linde, Migé and Ville and enabled the HIM boys to explore a new, heavier, sonic direction*

at our rehearsal room smoking pot many years ago'), Mige was 'Bad Migé Amour' and Ville 'Rakohammas'. Daniel Lioneye's backing band, the Rollers, was rounded out by HIM's lighting engineer Ilkka Kuusimäki (Ike) and producer Hiili Hiilesmaa (a.k.a. Dr. Skrepper), who provided backing vocals, keyboards and sound effects.

Produced by Hiili and released by BMG under their Oskon Records imprint, *The King Of Rock'n Roll* would become available in September 2001. A nine-track day-trip to the heavier end of the rock spectrum, *The King Of Rock'n Roll* sees Linde, Ville and Mige kicking out the jams across a series of numbers such as the album's engagingly daft title track. The song features lyrics like, 'I'm gonna give you what you need/I'm gonna make your ears bleed,' delivered in an Elvis-eque manner by Linde/Daniel, while Ville/Rakohammas contributes some spectacular drum fills. Asked about his bandmate's drumming abilities as part of an online fan Q&A, Gas was generous with his praise: 'I think that he's good. He's got a good groove and he plays really tasty drum parts. Although I think that he could hit them suckers a little bit harder though.' 'The King of Rock'n Roll' tickled the fancy of Bam Margera, who had established his reputation for brainless fun as part of the *Jackass* team, and selected the track as the theme music for his subsequent MTV show *Viva La Bam*.

Aside from a thunderous, distortion-laden, metal reworking of Bob Dylan's 'Knockin' On Heaven's Door', the remainder of *The King Of Rock'n Roll* comprises entirely original material, the pick of which are Linde's personal favourite, the blistering 'International P-Lover' ('P' in this instance standing for 'pussy') and the Aerosmith/Led Zep/Sabbath acid blues of 'Roller'. In keeping with their thoroughly rockin' sound and image, Daniel Lioneye took the opportunity to perform at a trio of Finnish outdoor shows during the summer, appearing at the Ilosaarirock and Tuska festivals in July, and Vantaa's Ankkarock event the following month.

*We're not a democratic band in the actual sense, but everyone has his job. I'm the asshole, Lily Lazer the drunk bastard and Mige the comedian. – **Ville Valo***

Never outdone, Gas kept busy with his own side-projects: a Motörhead and Entombed-influenced trio called Bendover ('it's really heavy shit we are talking about. And if the music is heavy, so are the guys. There is a weight limit of 100kg in the band,') and Äfäritila, a hardcore punk quartet that featured vocalist Lazze, who had established a reputation throughout mainland northern Europe from his twenty-year stint as vocalist with well-respected Finnish hardcore band Riistetyt. Burton, meanwhile, severed his ties with Sub-Urban tribe and Torpedo which, although difficult, was a necessary step, given HIM's forthcoming touring and promotional schedule.

HIM reconvened with another surprise gig at the Tavastia on 25 May 2001. Billed as Thulsa Doom, they supported local gothic garage combo The 69 Eyes. The two groups had a close relationship – Ville had provided backing vocals and appeared in The 69 Eyes' 'Wasting The Dawn' video and HIM's sound engineer, Janne Vuori, was the brother of Eyes frontman Jussi 69.

Aside from some minor issues concerning the sleeve art and track listing, the extended production process for the third album was at an end by the time HIM began making their usual round of summer festival appearances. The run of shows kicked off at the Rock am Ring event on 2 June, with a memorable performance that saw Ville framed as a windswept elfin Heathcliff beneath the darkening Teutonic sky. 'It was one of my first gigs in such a big place,' recalled Burton. 'We hadn't practised a lot before the gig. We had like two or three practice hours and they were without Ville.' Following a second appearance at the Rock im Park festival the following day, the band performed at outdoor events in Austria, Estonia, Russia, Switzerland and Turkey over the next three weeks.

Another town, another hotel – HIM check in on tour.

On 27 June 2001, the first results of HIM's studio labours were made public with the release of a new single. 'Pretending', an anthemic statement of what could be expected from the new LP, was released in Finland and Germany. The single was issued in a number of formats containing additional tracks and alternate versions of the main song and promoted via a fairly undistinguished video by former 10cc drummer/vocalist/beard Kevin Godley, which saw the band perform the song within an anonymous brutalist structure and was mainly notable for some vertigo-inducing camera work. Once again, the single climbed to the top of the Finnish chart and hit the Top Ten in Germany.

July saw HIM make their only Finnish festival appearance of the year, at the Ruisrock event in the historic administrative city of Turku. The following month, the group travelled to Hungary for a return to the Sziget festival, where they had debuted the

previous year. This was followed by a memorable day at the Viva Comet Awards in Germany, where the group received the 'Viewer's Choice' award, presented by the epitome of rock'n'roll wasted cool, Iggy Pop. 'I was so nervous I thought I was going to die but I didn't and I even got him to sign my *Naughty Little Doggie* vinyl,' gushed Linde, a huge Iggy fan. 'He also drew himself a Hitler moustache on the cover.' Ville was equally delighted at meeting the legendary Stooges frontman. 'He's always been an idol to me – he was great. He was a total gentleman and told us lots of stories about Finland because he's been there a couple of times. It's always great to meet your idol especially when they don't disappoint you.'

My lyrics are personal therapy, I'm saving a little money here. Actually I'm making a little. – Ville Valo

On 19 August 2001, HIM played their first ever concert in the USA at an X-Games preview for the skateboard stunt movie *CKY3* at the Trocadero Theatre in Philadelphia, which included a clip from the 'Right Here In My Arms' video directed by Bam Margera. The *Jackass* mainstay had been a huge fan of the band since a visit to Finland the previous year. 'He came to Finland for a skateboard show and he saw my face on the front of every fucking magazine so he bought the album [*Razorblade Romance*] and he fell in love with that,' explained Ville. 'Then we met in London and after that we'd see each other around and we'd be like drinking buddies and good friends.' The show closed with a performance of 'Rebel Yell', which was subsequently included on the DVD of *CKY3*.

Almost a year in the making, *Deep Shadows And Brilliant Highlights* hit the stores on 27 August. Aside from 'Pretending', the album featured nine more original compositions that took HIM's sound to a new plane. Opening with the subtle, multi-textured 'Salt In Our Wounds', the album clearly demonstrated how the relentless touring schedule and hundreds of rehearsal and recording hours had honed the band's technical interaction. Each song was a symbiotically balanced whole, combining each member's talents in the most effective manner.

Selected as one half of the double A-sided second single from *Deep Shadows . . .* 'Heartache Every Moment' exotically explores the exquisite anguish of forbidden love amidst a swirling, hypnotic whirl of anthemic guitar and piano. The song would later be included in the Bam Margera-directed *Haggard: The Movie* (2003), which starred Ryan Dunn (previously best known for inserting a toy car into his rectum on *Jackass*) as a jilted lover in a based-on-a-true-story tale of love and skateboarding in which Margera appeared as a character named 'Valo'.

'Lose You Tonight' is another track that indicates the way in which HIM now used the recording studio as an instrument in its own right: the electronic effects and

Band of brothers – after cutting a swathe across Europe, HIM fixed their sights on the USA in 2001.

Even at school I studied ethics instead of religion.
– Ville Valo

Two faces of Ville: The frontman charms another admirer (above) and in more reflective mode (right).

2001's Deep Shadows And Brilliant Highlights *saw the band move closer to the mainstream, hitting the Top Ten in several European countries.*

tonally rich production combine with the more traditional musical elements to pitch the listener into Ville's emotional maelstrom as he desperately attempts to prevent the departure of the object of his affections. This is another song included on the *Haggard* soundtrack.

Another future single, 'In Joy And Sorrow' is a lilting affirmation of enduring love that showcases Linde's sensitive lead to heartrending effect, and features what is possibly Ville's finest vocal performance on the album. The mantra-like quality of the chorus is given additional impact with each subtle variation of Ville's delivery, as the song builds to a sensitive climax.

After 'Pretending', the second half of *Deep Shadows . . .* begins with 'Close To The Flame' – the track selected to join 'Heartache Every Moment' on the band's January 2002 single. A fragile, entrancing exercise in sweet musicality and lyricism that is again dominated by Ville's intimate vocalisations, it has an ambiguous lyric, of which Ville observed, 'it can be a song about God if you want it to.'

'Please Don't Let It Go' finds producer Kevin Shirley combining a wide range of instrumental elements, which gather momentum to emerge as a standard – yet subtly complex – power ballad. This momentum combines with Ville's plaintive lyrics to produce a kind of emotive kinesis that modulates between longing and desperation. This process supercedes the simple meaning of the words and the conventional nature of the arrangement, hot-wiring the song's essence straight into the soul.

Like 'Close To The Flame', 'Beautiful' is a showcase for Ville's deeply personal vocal delivery, which dominates this shimmering, texturally rich exploration of the outer limits of love and desire. The rich, multi-layered production is indicative of *Deep Shadows*' quantum technical progression on its predecessors.

Women are always beautiful. – Ville Valo

'Don't Close Your Art' is another exercise in subtle smoke-and-mirrors atmospheric manipulation, representing the album's core theme – the parameters of death and love – as another accessible soft rock essay. 'These are the two themes about which people fantasise the most,' insisted Ville. This process, whereby similar themes are expanded and developed through subtle changes in presentation and delivery, reaches its conclusion with 'Love You Like I Do'. The organ-driven song is notable for Ville's dolorous vocals, an assertion of the unsurpassable strength of his feelings delivered at an almost funereal tone and tempo, as if struggling to escape the preceding tracks' gravity well of emotion. Easily the most experimental track on the album, it fades into entropy amid a corpus of gothic references such as clanging church bells and driving rain.

Within two days of its release *Deep Shadows And Brilliant Highlights* went gold in Finland and Germany, as well as hitting the Number 1 spot in Austria, Number 2 in Switzerland and cracking the Top 50 in Italy and Sweden. The disc even made a small dent in America, where it entered the lower reaches of the *Billboard* Top 200. Despite these successes, Ville was more concerned with maintaining the band's established fan base. 'Charts are not that important for us,' he asserted. 'It's important for us that the HIM fans we always had are content with us and our sound. People who know you just from the charts don't always go to your concerts.'

In addition to bringing the group to the attention of a wider demographic, HIM's chart profile drew increased media attention, the full glare of which was often directed at Ville, who had recently posed for a rock'n'roll calendar to raise money for a Finnish charity. 'I was called "The Sex God From *Sweden*" in a *Bravo* article,' marvelled the frontman. 'Anyway, all the members of the band are ironic people, so we don't take things too seriously.' With the core of the quintet founded on long-standing friendships, there was little chance that the media emphasis on Ville would have any detrimental effect on relationships within HIM. 'It's normal that most people are interested in the singer – and in this case the songwriter too,' Mige confirmed. 'If I were unhappy about it, I'd have to quit.'

Ville's reluctant elevation to sex symbol received further impetus as the band struck out in support of the new album in late 2001. With HIM taking in almost twenty European countries in less than three months, the tour was the biggest ever undertaken by any Finnish rock group, with audiences peaking at 10,000 in the largest venues. Although he admitted that 'playing live is still pretty difficult for me,' Ville had learned to accept the grimmer realities of life on the road. 'When it's good it's fantastic, but when it's not so good it's horrible. When people get ill on the tour bus, all of a sudden there's twelve people with diarrhoea and flu going round.'

I think Ville enjoys the things he's doing, also experimenting with make-up. Being a front man maybe means being vain. – Mige Amour

In October 2001, there was a brief two-week respite between the Swiss and Scandinavian legs of the tour, during which 'In Joy And Sorrow' was released as a single across continental Europe. The disc, which reached Number 2 in Finland and made the German, Greek and Portuguese Top Twenty, was accompanied by a video by John Hillcoat, who had directed the previous year's 'Join Me In Death' promo. This time around, the director framed a feline Ville and the band in muted sepia tones to create a visually literate tone poem of light and lost love. The release of the single during a break in the tour ensured the band were available for television appearances and interviews, which although a necessary part of the promotional circus that surrounds any successful band, would only serve to exacerbate feelings of exhaustion that they would experience at the tour's end.

The final night of the *Deep Shadows And Brilliant Highlights* European Tour came with a show at the Jubilenny Hall in St. Petersburg, Russia on 16 December 2001. After Christmas, the band briefly reconvened for their annual end of year gig at the Tavastia, before deciding to take a much needed break during the New Year. 'Basically, after the tour we were fucked,' revealed Ville. 'We didn't understand the fact that we'd been working for four years in a row without a proper holiday – so me, the ego-maniac and the wanker of the band, I was like almost on the verge of splitting up the whole thing on the tour because too much work makes Ville a really dull boy.'

Although the fatigue of touring had led to a number of disputes while the band were on the road, it would have been wastefully self-destructive for them to seriously consider splitting. Instead, they agreed to take a three-month break. Speaking in spring 2002 Ville observed, 'That break helped us out a lot in a way that [now] we're really energetic and feeling good about everything.'

Ville at the centre of things in leather, lipstick and eye-liner.

5 TIME ENOUGH AT LAST

We are like a very miserable version of the Backstreet Boys. – Ville Valo

For HIM, 2002 was a time of consolidation. While the band were taking their much needed two-month break, which saw Mige, Linde and Gas indulging in some recreational globetrotting while Ville stayed home with his guitar, the double A-sided 'Heartache Every Moment'/'Close To The Flame' was issued in Finland, Germany and Greece. The single was issued in a variety of formats, with one edition featuring acoustic versions of five tracks and videos of the two main songs on the disc. Such value-for-money marketing helped the single climb to Number 2 on the Finnish chart and penetrate the Top Twenty in Germany and Greece. Considering that this was the third single lifted from the previous summer's *Deep Shadows And Brilliant Highlights*, such sustained chart success of already available material clearly indicated HIM's audience was expanding.

This process continued with the UK release of *Deep Shadows And Brilliant Highlights* on 25 February 2002. To promote the album in Britain, and as a precursor to a more extensive tour later in the year, HIM touched down in London for a pair of shows: at the Barfly, and supporting legendary goth-rockers The Mission at the larger Astoria, drawing full houses (the Barfly sold out in two days) and universally positive reviews.

After a well-received run of Finnish club dates and an eight-gig tour of England and Scotland in the spring, HIM pared back their touring commitments to avoid the burn-out experienced at the end of the previous year and to begin preparations for a fourth album. With this in mind, the band only made nine festival appearances during the

Ville abandons his trademark long hair and woollen hat in favour of a more Byronic image.

summer – the most notable of which being an appearance at the fourth annual Obscuro Festival, which took place at the large Salón 21 ballroom in Mexico City on 31 August.

While HIM were making their Latin American debut, plans to launch the group north of the border hit a snag when it was discovered there was already an established American world music ensemble operating under the name of 'HiM'. The Chicago ensemble, formed by multi-instrumentalist Doug Scharin, were less than receptive to any requests to consider changing their name. 'I'm about to get embattled with the evil HIM – from Finland,' Scharin told *The Wire*'s Mike Barnes. 'They're sort of a Death Metal band, but it's a little more glam – they have songs like "Love Affair 666" and "Join Me In Death" and all this shit. And they're apparently really big in Germany. Their HIM stands for His Infernal Majesty. I'm seriously opposed to it, man, and as far as I can make out, we had the name first.'

> *We did some sports arenas but these are way too big for us – we're too inanimate ... We belong in shitty small clubs. – Ville Valo*

With the American band refusing to budge, Universal Records – who were keen to sign a US licensing deal with Ville and the band – issued a limited run promotional disc of 'Join Me' with the band billed as 'HER'. Similarly, initial pressings of *Razorblade Romance* – released in the US on the Jimmy Franks Recording Company label, run by Bloodhound Gang frontman Jimmy Pop – also bore the feminine version of the band's name. In November, Universal announced that they had signed the band to their Umvd imprint and gave *Razorblade Romance* a full release in October 2003, with new editions of *Deep Shadows And Brilliant Highlights* and *Greatest Love Songs 666* following in August 2004 and September 2005. In March 2003, a settlement was reached with HiM, who became 'American HiM' and all subsequent US releases by the Finnish quintet cited the band's correct name. 'The problem has been solved in an easy way,' explained Ville. 'We gave them money and made them happy.'

Aside from a surprise show at the Tavastia where HIM, billed as Black Salem, supported Hiili Hiilesma's garage punkabilly outfit the Skreppers on 7 September 2002, the Mexico City gig would be the last time the band appeared live until their annual New Year's Eve concert. On 16 September HIM checked into Finnvox to begin recording their fourth album, a process that would take almost three months to complete.

Initially, Finnvox's Mikko Karmila was mooted as a potential producer of the album, but with the band seeking to emphasise the heavier tones of their musical

Live and direct – Ville rocks another stadium.

I'm a huge fan of James Dean, that got me started.
*Nowadays I smoke four packs in a day. – **Ville Valo***

spectrum, Hiilesma was selected to man the desk. 'We decided that this album should be oriented on guitars,' recalled Ville. 'So we decided to take Hiili as the producer. Basically because there is nobody who's better in producing that way. Several years ago we recorded an album with him and his evolution during that time is quite big. That's the reason why we also used his studio in Helsinki as we didn't want him to work in a studio he doesn't know. It has become a second home for us.'

Given that Ville had been working on new songs for the follow up to *Deep Shadows And Brilliant Highlights* since early the previous year, there was little shortage of material from which selections could be made for the final track listing. This, allied to the close relationship between band and producer and the familiarity of their surroundings, ensured that the making of this album was far less fraught than the interminable process that bedevilled its predecessor. 'It was more natural, well rehearsed and more relaxed,' observed Linde.

Once the album was recorded, the masters were shipped to Scream Studios in Los Angeles, best known for playing host to the recording of Nirvana's *Nevermind* in 1991. There, former U2, Pearl Jam and INXS producer Tim Palmer set to work on mixing the ten selected tracks. 'Tim did a beautiful job unearthing all those hidden treasures within our music,' beamed Ville. 'I could just sit back wearing those fly glasses that Bono had left behind at the studio, and listen to the music sort of unravelling before my ears.'

With the new album not scheduled to hit stores until late the following spring, BMG issued a bumper ten-disc box set retrospective on 7 October. *The Single Collection* contains 44 radio edits, remixes and live tracks alongside all the group's previous singles save for 'Your Sweet 666'.

On 15 December 2002, HIM made their way to the historic LA Theatre to shoot a video for one of the stand-out tracks from the forthcoming album, 'Buried Alive By Love'. The song was selected for filming by Bam Margera, his favourite from the songs included on the new disc. The shoot was lent additional glamour by *Cape Fear* and *Natural Born Killers* star Juliette Lewis, who appears in the video as a sultry, Ville-struck rock chick. Margera had got to know Lewis through his friendship with the actress' former husband, professional skateboarder Steve Berra, and invited her to take part. The director then asked the group the largely rhetorical question: 'Is it OK if Juliette Lewis is in the video?'

The decision to issue 'The Funeral Of Hearts' as the first single from the new album necessitated a further video shoot, which took place under the aegis of Finnish polymath Stefan Lindfors, who had previously designed everything from wallpaper to restaurant interiors before branching out into film, with a short for telecommunications operator DNA in 2002. Shot in Finnish Lapland, Norway and the Southern Finnish towns of Porkkala and Hyvinkää, the shoot featured a smorgasbord of Nordic and elemental symbolism – funeral pyres, elves, mysticism and shape-

I think if we keep doing good music and people like us and they buy the magazine because we are in the magazine then they can't basically hate us hopefully...
— Ville Valo

changing beneath the big sub-arctic sky – and went on to win a *Kerrang!* award for best video.

Away from the constant treadmill of touring, recording and promotional duties that had engulfed HIM, Linde experienced some personal delight in March when his partner Manna gave birth to their daughter, Olivia, on 6 March 2003. Olivia arrived around three and a half weeks early, which meant that the guitarist had to rush home from England, where the band were set to appear on *Top Of The Pops* ahead of the release of 'The Funeral Of Hearts'. 'It was very important for me to be there,' beamed the proud father. 'I can't even begin to describe how fantastic it is – it's divine, it's a miracle! I'm the happiest man on earth!'

I love hearts. They are symbols for life, love and humanity. – Ville Valo

There was little rest for Linde, who travelled to Hamburg the following day for a special concert previewing the new album. The show at the Grosse Freiheit Club was intended as an opportunity for a thousand lucky fans, who had obtained tickets from the HIM website, to get an early taste of the material on the new disc. Before the show Ville admitted to being nervous, before adding, 'We're all anxious to see how the audience will react . . . I'm very proud of this gig and even though I'm a survivor from a bad flu I couldn't miss this show. I think this is a great way to let the record company, media and fans listen to our album . . . and I really hope that it will impress everyone in the best way.'

He needn't have worried. From the moment the band took the stage and launched into album opener 'Buried Alive By Love', they were inundated by successively larger waves of frenzied approval from their faithful following, many of whom had travelled from Poland, Greece and Italy. After running through each of the ten new tracks, HIM ran through a selection of crowd-pleasing favourites such as 'Right Here In My Arms', 'Your Sweet 666' and 'Wicked Game' before topping a triumphant set with a powerful rendition of 'Join Me In Death'.

On 17 March, the wider public got their first hint of what could be expected from the fourth HIM album when 'The Funeral Of Hearts' was issued as a single. Described by Ville as 'Roy Orbison meets Simon and Garfunkel meets Megadeth', the song is an anthemic celebration of life's finite span. Drawing lyrical inspiration from memories of his grandmother's funeral, Ville explained, 'I just smelt the pancakes she made, I remembered the scent of the cigarettes she smoked and the sound of the slippers on the floor – all of the good things – and that's what "Funeral Of Hearts"

Ville – HIM's songwriting maestro in repose at the piano.

The Love Metal Archives Vol. 1 *DVD featured the band's heartagram logo in place of the now-customary cover shot of Ville.*

is all about. All things come to an end eventually anyway – you should be able to celebrate that rather than just being gloomy and using black lipstick.' The single returned HIM to the top of the Finnish charts and hit the Number 3 slot in Germany and Greece, as well as making significant dents on the Austrian, Swiss and Spanish Top 30s.

With expectation across Europe at fever pitch, *Love Metal* was released on 14 April 2003. The title of the album was a partially ironic definition of HIM, their influences and the need for the media to categorise the band aimed at answering persistent questions as to what 'Love Metal' actually *was*. What is 'Love Metal'? *This* is *Love Metal*. As if to underline the definitive nature of the album, instead of the usual image of Ville, *Love Metal*'s sleeve depicted HIM's symbol – the heartagram.

Essentially a conflation of the pentagram and a heart, the heartagram is a visual representation of the link between love and death that permeates much of the band's output. 'We have such terribly short memory spans that we couldn't possibly think of having individual symbols like Led Zep did,' laughed Ville. 'The heartagram stands for HIM as a band, as an entity. And for love metal in general.' The symbol was based upon the logo used by the Mehiläinen private health care company, which Ville had noticed several years earlier. 'I'd been taking the tram from the rehearsal place to my home and passing this sign; I think it came from there. I was just drawing, subliminally added one line to that symbol and it turned into a pentagram/heart sort of thing,' he explained. 'But it took me a long time to understand there had to be a circle around it, like in the pentagram or peace symbol. We didn't add the circle until *Love Metal*.'

Ville's simple graphic device caught on rapidly with HIM's fans and became a popular tattoo shared by the band and their hardcore following. 'I'm happy about it because, for me, the heartagram stands for something bigger than just a band,' observed Ville. 'It's like Masonic – you meet people all around the world having it somewhere on their bodies and it's like a secret kind of thing.' Subsequently, Bam Margera adopted the heartagram, sharing the licensing with HIM and including it on his skateboards and assorted merchandise.

Sonically, *Love Metal* represents a kind of reiteration of HIM's initial influences. 'Basically the idea with *Love Metal* was to rip off as many idols as we could,' grinned Ville. 'The album starts out with a track called "Buried Alive By Love", which is clearly influenced by "Search and Destroy" by Iggy Pop and the Stooges from *Raw Power* – that youthful, animalistic energy has been lacking from a couple of things that we've done.'

The only message we want to spread is: have a good time and escape this cruel world for a while. – Ville Valo

Described by Ville as 'one of the heaviest HIM tracks ever', 'Buried Alive By Love' announces the album with a 300-second burst of emotional power that loses none of its sensitivity by being wrapped in layers of pounding drums, churning guitar and synthesized squall. A concrete metaphor for 'Love Metal', the song brings lyrical sensitivity to heavy rock in a manner that manages to be both intimate and exciting.

After 'The Funeral Of Hearts', 'Beyond Redemption' is another signpost towards the way in which, throughout *Love Metal*, HIM reconfigure their wide palette of influences to create new forms. Burton's keyboards evoke Depeche Mode and Pink Floyd, Linde's guitar intimates a missing link between Chris Isaak and Megadeth, and Ville's vocal adds feeling and resonance to the beautifully combustible mix.

'Sweet Pandemonium' sees HIM bringing Black Sabbath to their dark banquet. Elements of Sabbath's 'War Pigs' and 'Iron Man' are spun through the band's postmodern pop culture atom-smasher, along with soaring vocals, chunky guitar blocks,

Ville to the fore – 'We're not a democratic band in the actual sense, but everyone has his job. I'm the asshole, Lily Lazer the drunk bastard and Migé the comedian.'

cut-outs and well-directed distortion, to produce a song with roots woven through-out the 40-year history of heavy metal, yet is somehow all HIM. 'The slow, tired sounding groove is totally new to us. We hadn't anything like that on our earlier records.'

> *I'm really happy that Gas likes the album – the last album, he was like, 'this is not metal, y'know – that's bad. I just want to record metal.' He's sort of like a simpleton, but a very loveable dude. I'm really happy that Gas is happy. – Ville Valo*

As a description of how love makes slaves of all lovers, 'Soul On Fire' echoes *Razorblade Romance*'s 'I Love You' and 'Our Diabolical Rapture' from HIM's debut album. Musically, the track utilises again the interplay between Linde's guitar and Burton's keyboards to create a robust framework over which Ville's vocals soar, finding inspiration in despair and strength in longing. Ville's lyrical deification of love is further extended by 'The Sacrament'. Presenting similar themes within a ballad, the track alternates between Linde, Mige and Gas's coruscating riffola and Burton's neo-classical keyboards. 'I asked him to make something in the style of Richard Wagner and he simply did it,' Ville recalled. Of all the songs on *Love Metal*, 'The Sacrament' is possibly the most effective example of the unique synthesis of driving rock and sensitive balladry which epitomises the 'Love Metal' sound. Again, the universality of the lyrical themes and the deceptive simplicity of the arrangement mean that musical genre boundaries are only relevant to HIM as constructs to be transcended.

'This Fortress Of Tears' juxtaposes the heaviness of Linde's Tony Iommi-inspired lead against simple piano chord progressions and subtle studio embellishments, to create another variation on the 'Love Metal' theme. 'Circle Of Fear' grabs a handful of goth influences from the HIM pick'n'mix store for further blending within the album's overall template. With a chorus pedal lead guitar evocative of mid-period Siouxsie and the Banshees and vocals and bass direct from the Mission, this track bathes Ville's lyrical obsessions in reflected dark light.

The final two tracks on *Love Metal* represent an epic culmination of the musical and stylistic elements combined throughout the album. 'Endless Dark' superficially appears to be a straight-ahead rocker, whereas repeated listenings reveal layers of influences, evoking anyone from Neil Young to Cat Stevens to Bon Jovi. 'It's aggressive in a sentimental way,' explained Ville. 'We've gone back to our roots – just having fun like a garage band.' 'The Path' is a monumental slice of lavish, improvisational brilliance that references the group's stoner rock influences and allows each member of the band to enjoy a moment of prominence – a fitting way to end the album. 'It's a great introduction to popular music if you don't have the money to buy all of the Black Sabbath albums, every Elvis Presley album, all the Cat Stevens, Neil Young, Iggy Pop, eighties stuff like W.A.S.P., Twisted Sister, Iron Maiden, all that – it's all in there,' surmised Ville.

Although heavier than *Deep Shadows And Brilliant Highlights*, *Love Metal* proved to be no less commercial, topping the charts in Finland, Germany and Greece, making the Top Ten in Switzerland and Austria and achieving respectable placings in Italy, Norway and Sweden. The album was also HIM's first entry onto the British chart, where it peaked at Number 55. 'I don't think the fact that we are heavier now has any influence on the sales figures,' asserted Ville. 'If you notice the charts for the last year you can see that Slipknot are in the top position – I think it's a sign that the boundaries between different styles of music are more and more open.'

To announce the album's arrival, HIM arranged an unprecedented run of seven consecutive nights at the Semifinal Club at the end of April, tickets for which sold out within three hours of going on sale. The shows were recorded for inclusion on a live album with the projected title of *Live Metal*. However, due to the complexities surrounding various release dates of *Love Metal* and the band's back catalogue, plus a planned 'Greatest Hits' collection, these recordings remained in the vaults for almost a year.

To help promote the UK release of 'Buried Alive By Love', HIM played a one-off show at the Astoria on 3 May 2003. The gig had sold out six weeks in advance and the single, which was issued in three formats, pierced the British Top 30. Later in the year, the song would be re-issued with an exclusive live version of Black Sabbath's 'Hand Of Doom' recorded at the Rusirock Festival in Turku. This edition made the charts in Germany, Greece, Austria and Switzerland.

After a 17 May concert at Moscow's Maxidrome, HIM embarked on a circuit of selected summer festivals, designed to maximise their profile without causing the on-the-road burn-out that had afflicted the group two years earlier. On 31 May 2003, HIM made their debut at the Donnington Park Download Festival, which was headlined by Iron Maiden and Marilyn Manson. Ville and company appeared in a late afternoon slot on the second stage, between US metallers Soil and British psychedelic rockers Reef. 'It was a terrible hassle,' admitted Ville. 'because the previous night we were playing Madrid around midnight and we had about an hour's worth of sleep, then we had to be on the plane, straight to the gig, and then to London for some promotion stuff – we got to see a bit of Marilyn Manson on the screens backstage.'

A week later, HIM again found themselves sharing a bill with Marilyn Manson at the A Day At The Border festival in Monza, Italy. Like HIM, Manson's music set him outside the mainstream, leather-bristles-studs-and-acne approach to heavy metal,

*Many people think we are a bad band.
But we aren't. We kiss babies in front of cameras,
we are giving autographs – if we must, even
on the penis. – **Ville Valo***

Axe attack – Migé and Linde rock out.

Snapshot of a charismatic frontman – Ville's effect on his adoring audience is evident here.

which Ville saw as good news: 'the headliner is Marilyn Manson and I don't think that they are "heavy metal", so probably the audience will react in a positive way also to our music.'

On 16 June, 'The Sacrament' became the third single to be lifted from *Love Metal*. The accompanying video had been shot earlier in the year by Bam Margera at the Ploskovice Chateau, near Prague. A 'Love Metal' visual reworking of John Lennon's 'Imagine', the clip features Ville (with close-ups filmed at double speed to give a dreamlike slow-motion effect) wooing stunning Czech model Vanda Vosatkova, who Margera had discovered via a local model agency. The single went to Number 4 in Finland and made the German and Greek charts. It received a multi-format UK release in September and reached Number 27.

*We are a band similar to the Addams Family. We do what we want. We speak differently, we play differently and that's the difference. – **Ville Valo***

The remainder of the summer saw HIM visit Austria, Holland, Czech Republic, Germany, Denmark, Finland, Sweden, Greece, Portugal and Switzerland. After an appearance at the German Terremoto Festival on 29 August, the band took a break from the road ahead of a major bout of touring scheduled for the following year. 'This is the reason why we decided to release the record in April,' explained Ville. 'We're planning to do a big tour with more than one date in every area and in smaller clubs.'

As plans for a major UK tour supporting Ozzy Osbourne and an extensive run of gigs in Germany took shape, HIM returned from their six-week break to appear at the Senssi/Musiikki & Media Festival in Tampere on 17-18 October. On 9 December, Ozzy seriously injured himself in a quad biking accident, which necessitated the cancellation of his dates with HIM. Instead, the band organised their own mini-tour and gave their British fans a sneak preview of what to expect with another sold-out performance at London's Astoria on 19 December.

After the end-of-year holidays, which saw the band play their customary New Year's Eve gig at the Tavastia, HIM embarked on their most extensive programme of touring yet. Starting at Milan's Alcatrazz venue on 19 January, the band's 2004 itinerary would ultimately expand to encompass almost 100 shows. After one-off appearances in France and Luxembourg, the quintet played a run of five dates in Britain, all of which had sold out some weeks earlier. 'This is our third tour here,' Ville told the BBC. 'Back in 2000 we did the first one playing to 18-32 people and the next time around it was 200-300. Now there's clearly something wrong, there must be some sort of virus going round because suddenly we've become as successful as we are!'

Between a run of Spanish shows during February and the following month's German tour, BMG released HIM's cover of Neil Diamond's 'Solitary Man'. Once again Bam Margera directed the video, this time enlisting *Charmed* star Rose McGowan to appear as the kind of idealised, faithful woman that the song's lyrics are a paean to. The track was one of two new songs (along with 'And Love Said No') recorded in December 2003 for *And Love Said No: The Greatest Hits 1997-2004*. Like 'Wicked Game', 'Solitary Man' proved that a well selected cover version could break the band in new territories. In addition to topping the Greek chart and reaching Number 2 in Finland, the single became HIM's first Number 1 hit in Portugal, where it stayed on the chart for almost three months, and climbed as high as Number 6 in the UK.

You get your shit into the music and you can be a happy person outside of it, and eat ice cream and listen to the birds sing. – Ville Valo

And Love Said No: The Greatest Hits 1997-2004 was released on 15 March. The sixteen-track disc represented a handy way for new HIM fans to catch up on the band's back catalogue, and for the hardcore element, an enhanced edition featured half a dozen live tracks from the April 2003 Semifinal Club shows. 'Most people recognise the band from *Love Metal*. This compilation has got some of the older stuff too. It's for those who don't care about the band so much, but have heard the name or a few tunes,' observed Ville. 'That is all the singles we've released in Europe during the past seven years, it's sort of like getting that old stuff out to move on to new pastures.' The compilation topped the Greek chart, hit the Top Five in Finland and Germany, and established that HIM had a Canadian audience by scraping into the lower reaches of the national Top 100.

In mid-February, HIM announced that they would play a 22-date tour of the USA during April and May. The band's first string of concerts in the States would see them perform at a number of legendary smaller venues, such as the Bowery Ballroom in New York and the Whisky A Go Go on Sunset Boulevard, Los Angeles. Ville viewed the tour as a logical step in the band's climb toward total global domination, 'I've been laughing to myself that we've rehearsed for America in Europe for the past five years so I think we're ready . . . The world is such a big place that I'm really proud of our band taking these little baby steps,' he told *Modern Fix*'s Erin Broadley. 'Of course, I'm going to be disappointed if we're not the first band on the moon or if I'm

'Just one more question . . .' – Ville submits to another grilling on tour.

not going to be able to sleep in the same oxygen tent with Michael Jackson and Bubbles the monkey.'

HIM's American debut tour was an unqualified success, with all shows selling out and tickets changing hands for as much as $200 on the black market. 'Loads of kids knew all the lyrics to all the songs, even from albums that haven't been released here yet,' beamed Ville. 'It was really a big surprise for us. We thought we were going to have to go back in time – time travel – and start from scratch.'

After an all-too-brief fortnight off following their return from America in mid-May, HIM went straight out on the road again for the 2004 summer festivals. Aside from excursions to their fanbase hotbeds of Greece and Italy, the band confined their outdoor activities to Northern Europe. The centrepiece of these dates was a return to Donnington on 6 June, where they were scheduled to headline the second stage. However, a scheduling mix-up meant that HIM took the stage at the same moment that Metallica were playing on the main stage, and caused their set to be limited to a mere six songs. 'We were on the verge of not doing it at all,' admitted Ville. 'But we thought we would still play to the fans that wanted to see us. The times were altered because Slayer had problems with their technicians or something.'

The following day, HIM had a better time headlining the second annual *Metal Hammer* awards, where Ville carried off the Golden God for Best Rock Star prize and, along with Gas, entered into the true spirit of the occasion by staying up drinking until 9 a.m. the following morning.

After seeing out the festival season with appearances in Italy, Sweden, Finland, Greece and Switzerland, HIM took a break ahead of their most extensive UK tour to date, which was scheduled for October 2004. Never one to rest on his creative laurels, Ville provided backing vocals for a number of his friends' bands – along with Rasmus frontman Lauri Ylö^nen, he appeared on Apocalyptica's 'Bitter Sweet' single and also cropped up on recordings by the Skreppers, the 69 Eyes and Torpedo.

In September, the band signed a four-album contract with US label Sire. The deal included distribution rights worldwide, with the exception of Finland where the band would retain their own Heartagram imprint. The move from BMG was precipitated by uncertainty about a possible amalgamation with Sony. Sire, which had made its name in the 1970s-80s as the home for such diverse acts as Madonna, the Ramones and the Cure, triumphed in a bidding war that saw several major labels competing for HIM's signatures. A subsidiary of Warner, Sire had a track record of actively promoting bands and made a positive initial impression on Seppo: 'They show up to all the gigs, and in New York City they got the media on board, from *High Times* to the *New York Times*.' As a reaction to HIM's decampment, Universal gave *Deep Shadows And Brilliant Highlights* an unpromoted American release on 28 September. 'Even sold "cold" like this, it made it into the US Top 200,' observed Vesterinen.

To capitalise on their rising Stateside profile, HIM embarked on a second US tour in mid-November, the run of dates beginning just over a fortnight after the UK tour had climaxed with two sold-out shows at London's Hammersmith Apollo. Starting at the Worcester, Massachusetts on 12 November, the fourteen-date tour of club venues saw the band supported by stoner rock behemoths Monster Magnet, and former Hole and Smashing Pumpkins bassist Melissa Auf der Maur's eponymous solo project. 'The general idea is to keep things ticking over, to keep people aware of the band's existence before they take a break,' Seppo told *Helsingen Sanomat*'s Vesa Sirén. 'In the spring they will go into the studio to lay down a new album, and next fall it will be back to the States, perhaps as part of a larger tour package, for example Ozzfest or the Jägermeister Music Tour.'

Jesus was well into his thirties before he really did anything so I shouldn't be too worried. – Ville Valo

Although a resounding success, the tour reached a premature end when Ville's voice gave out due to a bout of laryngitis that necessitated the rescheduling of San Francisco and Los Angeles gigs for the following February. For Ville, such minor setbacks were all part of life on the road. 'Rock is all about touring and taking the music to the people rather than expecting the people to come to the band. Sometimes it's horrible, and sometimes it's beautiful – I can tolerate all the bad moments for those little moments of sheer beauty.'

2005 started with HIM taking part in a Red Cross benefit concert for victims of the recent Asian tsunami. The show, at the 12,500-capacity Hartwall Arena on 17 January, also featured the Rasmus, Apocalyptica, Negative and the 69 Eyes, and was broadcast live on national radio.

A fortnight later, *Love Metal* was given a full US release and rose to Number 117 on the *Billboard* Chart. HIM made a return to the States at the end of February to play the two concerts that had been cancelled in December. After their 27 February show at the Avalon in Los Angeles, the band checked into the Paramour Mansion at Silver Lake, east of Hollywood, to begin work on their fifth studio album. The 22-room estate had previously been a convent and a girls' school. More recently, a section of the complex had been converted into a studio, and the likes of Sting, Elton John and the Red Hot Chili Peppers had played concerts in the adjacent grounds.

Once again, Tim Palmer was selected to produce the album and was also responsible for recommending the mansion to HIM. 'Tim found us this beautiful mansion with a huge grand ballroom that is acoustically perfect because it was originally built for performances by opera singers,' Ville told *Metal Hammer*. 'You can see it in *Scream 3*. Playboy was filming here while we were recording. It was distracting for

Released in September 2005, Dark Light *became HIM's first album to crack the US Top Twenty.*

me to sing while watching all those silicone boobies.'

This time around, Ville and the band went into the studio with definite stylistic and conceptual ideas about what they wanted to achieve. 'I wanted them to be cool live songs, straight in the face kind of stuff. But it's really melodic at the same time,' explained the vocalist. 'It's crazy surreal, it's weird, it's David Lynch, it's Tim Burton, but with all those things happening within the AC/DC context. You can still shake your hips to it, bang your head, or play air guitar.'

Between the beginning of March and the end of May the group recorded fourteen songs, from which ten were selected for the album. The tracks that failed to make the final cut were a new version of 'And Love Said No', a cover of the Ramones' 'Poison Heart' and two new songs, 'Venus (In Our Blood)' and 'The Cage', which subsequently surfaced on the expanded limited edition release of the album. The LP took its title from another of Ville's new compositions, 'Dark Light': 'My last name; Valo, means "light" in Finnish. And the word "dark" if you translate it straight, it just means "the crazy being". Dark, in Finnish, meaning kind of "losing the plot". So it's kind of like a pun,' explained Ville. 'And "Dark Light" is nice because we had albums called *Deep Shadows And Brilliant Highlights* and *Razorblade Romance*, so we've always had these opposites.'

In between recording, Ville took the opportunity to give himself a quite dramatically short haircut. 'It was in bad condition and it looked horrible and I just cut it off back in the studio, nothing more. It's very simple indeed,' he told *HIM Online*.

Although the newly-shorn Love Metal Samson experienced an allergic reaction when he discovered a small pack of German Shepherd dogs inhabited the complex, he found the process of recording *Dark Light* far less stressful than had been the case with previous albums. 'It was actually the most relaxed time of making an album ever for us. We've been together more than ten years, and it was the first time that everyone seemed to enjoy recording.'

While HIM were recording *Dark Light*, Sony/BMG released *Love Metal Archives Volume 1*, an extensive DVD compilation that gathered together all of the band's videos – from the initial home movie version of 'Wicked Game' to 'And Love Said No' – over twenty live clips filmed between 1998 and 2004, and a host of interviews and other extras. The collection sold well, topping the music DVD charts in Finland and Britain and reaching Number 2 in Germany.

On 2 June 2005, the band surprised and delighted their German fan club with an unscheduled appearance at a meeting at the Backstage Club in Munich. The following day, they made their annual appearance at Rock Im Park and played Rock Am Ring two days later. HIM's 11 June mainstage performance at the Download festival (where they were third on the bill to Black Sabbath and reconstituted ex-Guns N' Roses 'supergroup' Velvet Revolver) was to be their last gig for almost a month. With extensive tour plans coming together in support of *Dark Light*, the Finnish fivesome pared back their summer festival commitments to a mere half-dozen shows, the final pair of which took the band to Japan for the first time to appear at the Tokyo and Osaka legs of the rolling Summer-Sonic event.

In addition to doing some filming with Bam Margera for his MTV show *Viva La Bam*, Ville's summer was notable for his engagement to girlfriend Jonna Nygren. Instead of a ring, Ville had the letter 'J' tattooed on his ring finger. 'We've known each other for years and years, and we've lived together for the past two years – it felt right,' he told *musicOMH.com*'s Chris Ingold.

HIM returned to intensive touring at the beginning of September, with a run of one-night stands in Germany, France, Slovakia, Italy, Spain, Holland and England. These shows coincided with the European release of 'Wings Of A Butterfly', the track selected to trail the forthcoming album. Described by Ville as 'really sweet and fucked up . . . philosophical, with a bit of Michael Jackson's "Billie Jean" in the verses,' the single was accompanied by the band's most dynamic video for some time. Directed by Meiert Avis – who had established a formidable reputation through his work with U2 and also made promos for Bruce Springsteen, Bob Dylan and Van Halen – the video transplants HIM to a dystopian near-future, based on the graphic motifs found throughout the *Dark Light* packaging. 'We didn't want to act and we didn't want to have ladies in the

113

video, because I think that's so boring – rock videos with a pretty chick doing nothing,' revealed Ville. 'Bam likes to do videos like that and it's been great fun, but you can only do it so many times otherwise it becomes terribly boring.'

'Wings Of A Butterfly' topped the Finnish chart and made the Top Ten in England, Germany and Spain, with respectable chart placings achieved throughout the continent. Less than a fortnight after the single was released, *Dark Light* hit the stores on 23 September 2005.

In addition to being their debut LP for Sire, the disc was HIM's first album to have something resembling a simultaneous global release, with the US edition coming out on 26 September. From the opening track, 'Vampire Heart', *Dark Light* is revealed as a culmination of HIM's development, taking their signature dark/light, soft/hard, metal/ballad dualism to a new plateau of accomplishment. 'Vampire Heart' alternates between thrash-metal riffola and sensitive balladry to diffuse new light through Ville's lyrical prism of desire and heartbreak.

This high-octane opening is maintained by the inclusion of 'Wings Of A Butterfly' (under its full title of 'Rip Out The Wings Of A Butterfly') as the disc's second track and continues into the infectious, 'Street Spirit'-inspired 'Under The Rose', Ville's evocation of doomed love in a cold climate, which culminates in a soaring middle eight. The song ends with a moody, electronica-infused coda, 'Kind of like Massive Attack on a *very* bad day,' joked Ville.

Destined to be the third single taken from *Dark Light*, 'Killing Loneliness' proved the most difficult of the ten tracks to record. 'We just couldn't get it right,' Ville admitted. 'We had the drum parts and we had the guitar parts but the keyboards and the vocals weren't there. It took us the entire two months for recording it and two or three months of rehearsals to finish it off.' It was worth all the hassle; the track is a haunting, melodic demonstration of the classic HIM style. Layers of guitars, keyboards, vocals and drums overlap to produce an aural atmosphere comprising multiple waves of sonic zephyrs, siroccos and tsunamis.

The album's title track provides Ville with a showcase for his vocal sensitivity. 'It's one for the ladies out there,' he observed. 'It's the most sentimental and poppy song on the whole album.' Musically, the track evokes Golden Globe-winning composer Angelo Badalamenti's score for David Lynch's *Twin Peaks* – which Ville was a huge admirer of.

Originally called 'Kajagoogoo', after the wimpy British eighties band of the same name – a reference to the song's 'slightly cheesy' intro – 'Behind The Crimson Door' is *Dark Light*'s goth track. Containing such characteristic Valo lyrics as 'Your love will be the death of me', the song gathers momentum as Linde's guitar gradually pushes its way to the fore, and barely audible spoken sections infuse the track with a sense of glowering mystery.

We're a Goth band, more or less, so be careful! We're super-miserable and super-mysterious. – Ville Valo

After opening with some pounding drum/guitar interplay, 'The Face Of God' drops down a gear to reveal itself as an ominous, mid-tempo, sample infused exploration of love gone awry that segues well into the subsequent 'Drunk On Shadows' – which explores similar lyrical themes within a framework of crystalline harmonies and churning bottom end guitar. 'It sounds like if the Beach Boys started playing heavy metal before Black Sabbath did,' Ville told *Kerrang!*

Dark Light's only proper ballad, 'Play Dead' makes effective use of haunting keyboards and dramatic bursts of guitar and drums to frame a twisted lullaby of love and regret. Ville's poignant lyrics are done full justice by what is perhaps his most accomplished vocal performance on the disc.

The album closes with the epic 'In The Nightside Of Eden', which features a choir, driving metal guitars, industrial sound effects, Rob Zombie-style closing vocals and references to Dante Aligheri and Aleister Crowley acolyte Kenneth Grant. Almost a throwback to the band's formative Lovecraft-influenced thematics, the song is a suitably grandiose conclusion to a monolithic representation of the HIM sound. Lyrically, the track explores elements of metaphysics, contrasting the physical and spiritual realms: 'it's about still having a dream but nobody knows what that dream is anymore,' explained Ville. 'It's just about the politics of the heart, but it's not political.'

The whole package came wrapped in a sleeve designed by Ville, which was the band's most extravagant yet. 'There's a big high-rise Gotham City kind of building with a HIM logo on top and then the windows being lit, or the only windows being lit form the heartagram, and then it's in the middle of a raging sea so it's like post-apocalyptic, like a *Day After Tomorrow* kind of thing,' he explained. 'We wanted it to be really cinematic, as the music is, so it looks more like a movie poster than an actual artwork for a rock band.'

As expected, *Dark Light* hit the top of the Finnish charts, going platinum within five days of its release. Similarly, the disc went Top Ten in countries such as Greece, Germany, Austria, Switzerland, Italy, Spain and Sweden where HIM had built up an enthusiastic following over the past eight years. What really demonstrated that the group had arrived as a global rock phenomenon were sales in the US, where the album reached Number 18, selling in excess of 500,000 copies by the end of September 2006. Almost as satisfying was the Top Twenty placing in England and Top Forty showings in Canada and Australia – two countries that the band had yet to tour.

With MTV picking up on the band's videos and the quintet's profile at an all-time high, HIM saw out 2005 with a rigorous two-month long North American tour. The trek included the group's 500th official gig at the Hub in Santa Barbara on 9 October, and saw the touring party cross the borders into Canada and Mexico as the roadshow meandered its way around the continent. For Ville, the band's US success was something of a double-edged sword. 'Touring in the States is a pain in the ass every now and then because the travel is really, really heavy, especially on this tour . . . The dis-

People think that rock is dead. But it has never gone away. – Ville Valo

Down in the pit – Migé and Ville get close to the crowd

tances are so long compared to Europe,' he told the *LiveMetal* website. 'With *Dark Light* being the first album properly released here, we have been doing some press for it and it's being played on the radio now, thank God. Of course it has changed the vibe. A lot more people know who we are.'

This time around, Ville's voice stayed the course and the only gig cancellations occurred in New Orleans, where the horrendous aftermath of Hurricane Katrina necessitated that the scheduled Voodoo Music Festival show be relocated to Memphis. However, Ville was finding that the tour was taking its toll; he was drinking heavily, suffering from panic attacks, his relationship with Jonna was becoming strained, and, after a Minneapolis show in October, he'd had his beer spiked with a date rape drug, and awoke to find his wallet, cell phone and asthma inhalers missing. 'When you decide to get totally fucked up in Minneapolis don't hang out with

We've been doing this for 10 years, I hope we can continue at least the next ten, too. – Gas Lipstick

random guys, because that's what I did and someone spiked my drink and stole everything,' he told *Kerrang!* 'Luckily nothing worse happened. I had a couple of scratches, probably from falling down, but nothing worse.' The incident caused Ville to reassess his drinking and he subsequently opted for a cautious policy of remaining sober. 'It felt weird at first but I'm fine now.'

HIM returned to Finland at the end of November and played their final gig of the year at the Tavastia on New Year's Eve. That year, HIM's traditional end-of-year club gig had expanded into a three-day mini-festival split between the Tavastia and SemiFinal clubs, and included performances from the 69 Eyes, Charon, Sunride, Negative, Bloodpit, Deep Insight, Bleak and Underdogs.

In January 2006, Linde slipped on an icy pavement after a New Year party and fractured his left wrist, putting the guitarist out of action for the whole of January and causing the group's planned UK tour to be rescheduled for April. This change of plan meant that HIM would now be on the road until mid-July without any substantial breaks.

On 11 January, 'Killing Loneliness' became, after the previous November's vinyl-only release of 'Vampire Heart', the third single to be lifted from *Dark Light*. The track was issued across Europe over three months, with the UK edition coming out as late as 24 April. In addition to making Number 2 in Finland, 'Killing Loneliness' again made the British and German charts and was promoted by a remarkable video directed by Noble Jones that depicted the band as the main attraction in a peep show.

Don't look back – Migé and Ville take a walk in the park.

The group's arduous global trek started in Russia in February, with the first of a run of shows with the Rasmus that would take them across mainland Europe. After the Athens gig on 13 March, HIM boarded a flight to Japan where they again visited Tokyo and Osaka, before travelling on to play four concerts in Australia and New Zealand. The rescheduled UK dates followed in mid-April and after their biggest British show to date at London's Brixton Academy on 25 April, the quintet hopped across to Dublin for a pair of appearances at the historic Ambassador Theatre. Despite this hectic schedule, Ville retained a sense of perspective regarding the arduous nature of touring, 'Every gig is very different, and you can't really pick like, the best one or the worst one,' he told Croatian TV. 'There are bad gigs, and there are good gigs, but usually, there is beauty in every gig, any one. And that difference is what makes it all interesting. We don't have any routine, like some dance bands or like some boy-bands, it's all pretty improvised.'

We're trying to have the band create something beautiful that hopefully one day, 20 years from now, can be picked up by a kid and hopefully have the same effect that Neil Young had on me, or Led Zeppelin or Black Sabbath. – Ville Valo

As the charismatic frontman for a band that were now selling out large venues across the globe, Ville was subject to something approaching worship from his growing legion of female fans. When asked about how he coped with such attention by the BBC, he gave a typically level-headed response. 'It's cool that people are interested in what we do but that's about it. It's funny, we're honoured and we keep on blushing every time we see all those people screaming at us.' Similarly, the vocalist also found himself portrayed as a sex symbol by the press. 'I'm always in the same "sex symbol" category as Marilyn Manson and Mortiis, so make your own conclusion,' observed the unruffled vocalist.

After a second US tour in six months that took up much of May and June, HIM returned to Europe for a limited run of eight summer festival appearances. A projected fall tour of America was cancelled in September, as the group felt that they had spent too much time on tour and too little in the studio. 'We just want to keep it fresh for you and stump you with new material,' announced Ville. 'I didn't feel that I could do that without rehearsing some of this stuff that's stuck in my heart. We're happy to have new fans come aboard the ship, but I feel we've got to keep it exciting and new. We've started writing and I can't wait for you guys to hear what we're working on.'

In October, Sony/BMG issued *Uneasy Listening Vol. 1*, the first of a projected two-volume edition rounding up fifteen alternate mixes, acoustic versions and demos from the HIM back catalogue. The album was not a huge success, containing too many songs that were already available in a wide variety of forms and consequently achieving only a moderate impact on the charts.

I like getting older. I hope I don't lose my hair before I turn 50. – Ville Valo

A difficult year ended for HIM with another mini-festival in Helsinki, which this time featured British bands Cathedral and Anathema alongside Sweden's Katatonia and a clutch of local Finnish bands. Ville was glad to see the back of 2006. Speaking to *Kerrang!*'s Tom Bryant in 2007, he observed, 'Last year was a mess. A lot of bad things happened – friends died or got terminally ill, lots of stuff like that. Trying to work while that's all happening is really hard. Your heart gets jaded.'

With HIM off the road and preparations for the next album being made at a relaxed pace, Ville and the band began to recover some of the energy that was exhausted during eighteen months of gigging and promotion. Burton was enjoying his new role as a father, and Ville's stress-induced panic attacks subsided.

Despite recent personal difficulties, Ville has much to look forward to – HIM are established as one of the planet's most in-demand rock bands and, with an imminent new album and a re-energised approach to touring, both the frontman and his four amigos are highly positive. 'I'm happy that four of my old school mates and friends are still in the band and that we can laugh, play cards on the tour bus and not mention the word money. We're all just big fans and lovers of music. That's beautiful. We've had bad moments with the band as well but that's how it always is with people you love. It's natural. But at this particular moment we're in really good shape and feeling good about the future.'

And so they should be. HIM are a unique phenomenon from a very singular background, who have delighted their thousands of fans with their highly individual contribution to the rock milieu. More than that, they have even managed to impress the usually phlegmatic Kari Valo, who declared, 'Maybe HIM is second to God – I'm very proud.'

Selected Discography

Singles/EPs

666 Ways To Love EP
Stigmata Diaboli/Wicked Game/Dark Secret
Love/The Heartless
BMG 74321 42452 2 – Finland
October 1996

Wicked Game/For You
BMG 74321 62463 2 – Finland
October 1996

When Love And Death Embrace (Radio
Edit)/When Love And Death Embrace
(Album Version)
BMG 74321 53088 2 – Finland
October 1997

Your Sweet Six Six Six/The Beginning Of
The End (Tandeberg B74 Mix)/The
Beginning Of The End (Satanik Love Mix)
BMG 74321 56152 2 – Finland
February 1998

Join Me In Death/Rebel Yell (Live)
BMG 74321 74552 – Finland
November 1999

Join Me In Death/It's All Tears (Drown In
This Love) (Unplugged)/Rebel Yell (Live)
BMG 74321 70453 2 – Germany
November 1999

Right Here In My Arms (Radio Edit)/Join
Me In Death (Razorblade Mix)/The
Heartless (Space Jazz Dubmen Mix)

BMG 74321 74857 2 – Germany
March 2000

Right Here In My Arms (Radio Edit)/I've
Crossed Oceans Of Wine To Find
You/Sigillum Diaboli
BMG 74321 74858 2 – Finland
March 2000

Poison Girl/Right Here In My Arms
(Live)/It's All Tears (Live)
BMG 74321 76735 2 – Finland, BMG 74321
77485 2 – Germany
July 2000

Gone With The Sin (Radio Edit)/For You
(Unplugged)/Gone With The Sin
(Orchestra Version)/Gone With The Sin
(Album Version)
BMG 74321 80000 2 – Finland
October 2000

Gone With The Sin (Radio Edit)/Gone
With The Sin (Orchestra Version)/For You
(Unplugged)/Bury Me Deep Inside Your
Heart (Live)/ Gone With The Sin (Album
Version)
BMG 74321 80350 2 – Germany
October 2000

Pretending (Radio Edit)/Pretending
(Alternative Mix)/Pretending (The Cosmic
Pope Jam Version)
BMG 74321 866449 2 – Finland
June 2001

Pretending (Radio Edit)/Pretending (Alternative Mix)/Pretending (The Cosmic Pope Jam Version)/Please Don't Let It Go (Acoustic Version)/Lose You Tonight (Caravan Version)
BMG 74321 87171 2 – Finland
June 2001

In Joy And Sorrow (Radio Edit)/Again/In Joy And Sorrow (String Version)
BMG 74321 89004 2 – Finland
October 2001

In Joy And Sorrow (Radio Edit)/Again/In Joy And Sorrow (String Version)/Salt In Our Wounds (Thulsa Doom Version)/Beautiful (Third Seal Version)
BMG 74321 89005 2 – Finland
October 2001

Heartache Every Moment/Close To The Flame/Salt In Our Wounds (Acoustic Version)
BMG 74321 91557 2 – Finland
January 2002

Heartache Every Moment/Close To The Flame/Salt In Our Wounds (Acoustic Version)/ In Joy And Sorrow (Acoustic Version)/ Pretending (Acoustic Version)/Heartache Every Moment (Acoustic Version)/ Close To The Flame (Acoustic Version)
BMG 74321 91558 2 – Finland
January 2002

The Funeral Of Hearts (Radio Edit)/The Funeral Of Hearts (Album Version)/ The Funeral Of Hearts (Acoustic Version)
BMG 82876 50480 2 – Finland, Sweden
March 2003

The Funeral Of Hearts (Radio Edit)/The Funeral Of Hearts (Album Version)/ The Funeral Of Hearts (Acoustic Version)/Soul On Fire (Erich Zann's Supernatural Remix)/The Funeral Of Hearts (Dr. Dagon's Dub Remix)

BMG 82876 50481 2 – Finland
March 2003

Buried Alive By Love (Radio Edit)/Wicked Game (Radio Edit)/I've Crossed Oceans Of Wine To Find You
BMG 82876 52316 2 – UK, Ireland
May 2003

Buried Alive By Love (Radio Edit)/Join Me (Razorblade Mix)/Rebel Yell (Live)
BMG 82876 52318 2 – UK, Ireland
May 2003

The Sacrament (Radio Edit)/Buried Alive By Love (Live)/The Sacrament (Acoustic Version)
BMG 82876 52913 2 – Finland
June 2003

The Sacrament (Radio Edit)/Buried Alive By Love (Live)/The Sacrament (Acoustic Version)/Buried Alive By Love (Deliverance Version)/The Sacrament (Disrhythm Remix)
BMG 82876 52913 2 – Finland
June 2003

The Sacrament (Radio Edit)/Sigillum Diaboli/One Last Time
BMG 82876 55880 2 – UK, Ireland
September 2003

The Sacrament (Radio Edit)/Again/In Joy And Sorrow (String Version)
BMG 82876 55889 2 – UK, Ireland
September 2003

Solitary Man/Please Don't Let It Go (Live)/Join Me In Death (Live)
BMG 82876 60107 2 – Germany
March 2004

And Love Said No (Radio Edit)/It's All Tears (Live)/Pretending (Live)
BMG 82876 62389 2 – Finland
July 2004

Wings Of A Butterfly/Poison Heart
Sire 054391591821 – UK, Ireland
September 2005

Wings Of A Butterfly/And Love Said No
(616 Version)/Vampire Heart (Live)
Sire 093624282624 – UK, Ireland
September 2005

Vampire Heart (Single sided 7" silver vinyl
limited edition)
Sire W697 – UK
November 2005

Killing Loneliness/Rip Out The Wings Of A
Butterfly (Live)/Play Dead (Live)
Sire 64300224400108 – Finland
January 2006

Killing Loneliness/The Cage (Album
Version)/Rip Out The Wings Of A Butterfly
(Live)/Under The Rose(Live)
Sire 093624288920 – Germany
February 2006

In Joy And Sorrow (String
Version)/Pretending (Acoustic Version)
RCA 88697 02895 28 – Finland
November 2006

Studio Albums

Greatest Lovesongs Vol. 666
Your Sweet 666/Wicked Game/The
Heartless/Our Diabolikal Rapture/It's All
Tears (Drown In This Love)/When Love
And Death Embrace/The Beginning Of The
End/(Don't Fear) The Reaper/For You/Dark
Circle 66
BMG 74321 53106 24 – Finland
November 1997

Razorblade Romance
I Love You (Prelude To Tragedy)/Poison
Girl/Join Me In Death/Right Here In My
Arms/Gone With The Sin/Razorblade
Kiss/Bury Me Deep Inside Your

Heart/Heaven Tonight/Death Is In Love
With Us/Resurrection/One Last Time
BMG 74321 73221 20 – Finland
January 2000

Deep Shadows And Brilliant Highlights
Salt In Our Wounds/Heartache Every
Moment/Lose You Tonight/In Joy And
Sorrow/Pretending/Close To The
Flame/Please Don't Let It
Go/Beautiful/Don't Close Your Heart/Love
You Like I Do
BMG 74321 87749 28 – Finland
August 2001

Love Metal
Buried Alive By Love/The Funeral Of
Hearts/Beyond Redemption/Sweet
Pandemonium/Soul On Fire/The
Sacrament/The Fortress Of Tears/Circle Of
Fear/Endless Dark/The Path
BMG 82876 50501 28 – Finland, Germany,
UK
April 2003

Dark Light
Vampire Heart/Rip Out The Wings Of A
Butterfly/Under The Rose/Killing
Loneliness/Dark Light/Behind The Crimson
Door/The Face Of God/Drunk On
Shadows/Play Dead/In The Nightside Of
Eden
Sire 09362 49284 23 – Finland, Germany,
UK, USA
September 2005

Compilations and collections

And Love Said No – The Greatest Hits 1997-2004
And Love Said No/Join Me/Buried Alive By
Love/Heartache Every Moment/Solitary
Man/Right Here In My Arms/Funeral Of
Hearts/In Joy And Sorrow/Your Sweet
666/Gone With The Sin/Wicked Game/The
Sacrament/Close To The Flame/Poison

Girl/Pretending/When Love And Death
Embrace
BMG 82876 60040 21 – Finland, Germany
March 2004

Uneasy Listening Vol. 1
The Sacrament (Disrhythm Mix)/The
Funeral Of Hearts (Acoustic Version)/Join
Me In Death (Strongroom Mix)/Close To
The Flame (The Rappula Tapes)/In Joy And
Sorrow (String Version)/It's All Tears
(Unplugged Radio Live)/When Love And
Death Embrace (AOR Radio Mix)/Buried
Alive By Love (Deliverance Version)/Gone
With The Sin (O.D. Version)/Salt In Our
Wounds (Thulsa Doom Version)/Please
Don't Let It Go (Acoustic Version)/One
Last Time (Rockfield Madness version)/For
You (Unplugged Radio Live)/The Path (P.S.
Version)/Lose You Tonight (Thulsa Doom
Extended Dub)
Republic 88697 01168 24 – Finland,
Germany
October 2006

Uneasy Listening Vol. 2
Buried Alive By Love (616 Version)/
Rendezvous With Anus (el Presidente
Version)/Sigillum Diaboli (Studio Live
Evil)/I Love You (White House
Version)/Beginning of The End (Sad Damn
Version)/Again (Hollovlad Tapes)/Wicked
Game (Live In Turku)/Soul On Fire (Erich
Zann's Supernatural Remix)/Beautiful
(Hollovlad Tapes)/Endless Dark (616
Version)/Hand Of Doom (Live In
Turku)/Right Here In My Arms (Live In
Turku)/Sailin' On (Live In
Turku)/Pretending (Cosmic Pope Jam
Version)
Republic 000901402 – Finland, Germany
May 2007

ACKNOWLEDGEMENTS

A number of magazines, news and music papers were consulted during the writing of this book. These include: *Bravo, Demi, Divine, Freies Wort, Kerrang!, Ilta-Sanomat, Loud, Mädchen, Metal Hammer, Metal Heart, New Musical Express, New Rhythm, Orkus, Popcorn, Rennbahn Express, Rock Hard, Rock & Pop, Rock Sound, Sonic Seducer* and *Supersonic*.

There are a number of websites providing useful information about the HIM. The most interesting and informative include: *heartagram.com, him666worship.cjb.net, himsanctuary, himonline.tv, ofabutterfly.com, vampireheart.altavista.org, funeralofhearts.com, h-i-m666.com, thesacrament.net, heartagram.info, hhs.wcs.k12.va.us,home.arcor.de/aegypten22/musik/him* and *rockdetector.com*

A number of people deserve thanks for their invaluable assistance, without which this book would have proven impossible to write: Taina Franzen and Seppo Vesterinen of HIM Management for their help and assistance, Anna Jones for her essential advice, Spröet Weintraub, Roman Totale for their support, assistance and inspiration. Finally thanks to Ville Valo and his band, Emerson Burton, Migé Paananen, Linde Lindström and Gas Lipstick who gave us inspiration.

We would like to thank the following photographers who gave us much help in the production of this book. Their pictures appear on the following pages:

Tobias Seeliger: pages 16, 25, 32, 35, 38, 41, 75, 81, 82, 84, 85, 93, 105, 106, 109, 114, 117, 119, 121.
Jouko Lehtola: pages 5, 26, 28, 31, 53, 55, 66, 72, 73, 89, 94, 95, 102.
Nauska: pages 6, 20, 23, 37, 43, 46, 56, 57, 61, 62, 69, 77, 97.
Paul Harries: cover and pages 90, 99, 122.
www.paulharries.com
Brian Rasic: pages 8, 44, 71.
Sakari Viika: pages 13, 15.
Vertti Teräsvuori: page 18.